LOW CALORIE MENUS
for Entertaining

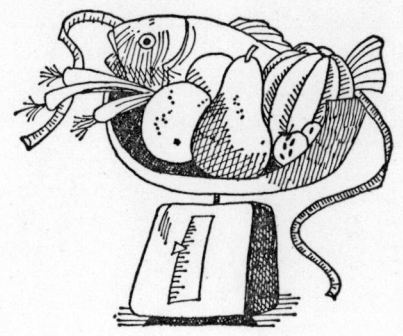

LOW CALORIE MENUS
for Entertaining

WITH RECIPES AND MENUS FOR
Protein Diets / Starch Diets / Sweet Diets

by Elaine Ross

Edited by Inez M. Krech
Illustrations by Loretta Trezzo

HASTINGS HOUSE · PUBLISHERS
NEW YORK

Copyright © 1970 by Elaine Ross

All rights reserved. No part of this book
may be reproduced without
written permission of the publisher.

Published simultaneously in Canada by
Saunders, of Toronto, Ltd. Don Mills, Ontario

Printed in the United States of America

CONTENTS

Introduction	6
Protein Diet Breakfasts	11
Starch Diet Breakfasts	12
Sweet Diet Breakfasts	13
Harmless Nibbles	14
Special Treats	15
Protein Lunches	16
Starch Lunches	34
Sweet Lunches	56
Protein Dinners	76
Starch Dinners	122
Sweet Dinners	168
Calorie Tables	207
Index	213

INTRODUCTION

In 1952, a young woman lost forty-five pounds. A year later, *Reduce and Enjoy It Cookbook* was published. A career was launched.

Seventeen years later, the score shows five cookbooks and countless magazine articles published. The young woman, now a grandmother, still holds her own on the scale. The career has expanded to include some teaching and lecturing, some work as a food consultant. The seventeen years have been gratifying and exciting.

Too, the svelte grandmother earned a reputation for setting an uncommonly good table. When friends came to dinner, they expected something different, something special, and they were rarely disappointed. But, though the "party" dishes in my home have tasted rich, generally they were not. I do not mean that the recipes were decalorized completely, but the proportion of rich ingredients was streamlined, as long as streamlining did not detract from flavor. (For example, I make a streamlined sauce base using one tablespoon of butter to two tablespoons of flour instead of the usual equal quantities. Much less rich, and tastes just fine. Or, I streamline whipped cream by folding in stiffly beaten egg white just before serving. There are myriad tricks.) Not all recipes can be edited and streamlined. I have culled my files and have chosen the most adaptable for this book.

All well and good. I am in control when the parties are in my home, but what about my invitations to friends' homes? In an effort to reciprocate handsomely, they treat me to an avalanche of butter and whipped cream and chocolate, confusing rich cooking with fine cooking. In self-protection I learned to make an educated estimate of the calories on a buffet table or a platter, and helped myself accordingly.

Every hostess watched carefully for my seal of approval on each mouthful. It took sleight of hand to convince her that I had helped myself lavishly and licked the platter clean. Yet, had I done that, I should certainly have been back where I started in very short order. My friends would have been quick to report the least change in me, particularly in the neighborhood of my hips. It would hardly do to have the author of *Reduce and Enjoy It Cookbook* look like the best possible candidate for her own book.

This book is for the hostess. It is also for the guest. It is aimed at those who enjoy fine food and to whom weight maintenance or weight reduction is a problem (which means almost everyone). It is designed to help the hostess serve mouth-watering meals to her guests without penalizing them weightwise. It is for the guest who is learning what to eat and where to hold back when invited out. (Why do I always think that the smallest things have the most astronomical number of calories? As a matter of fact, an analysis of many hors-d'oeuvre and *petits fours* will bear me out. You can often help yourself more safely to a sandwich or dessert.)

There isn't any magic formula to weight control. It all boils down to simple arithmetic—the addition of calories. I haven't found any abracadabra that will permit weekend feasting at friends' homes and in restaurants without that grim Monday morning confrontation with the scale. Then, the vow that today, this morning, from this moment on, the goodies will be minimal. And, so they probably will—until the next weekend.

This is not a diet book one would use to effect a rapid or substantial loss of weight. It is rather a guide to eating wisely and well, particularly when you are planning a party or going to one. And, if you follow these menus and recipes, you will probably lose a pound or two or even more despite yourself.

As I said, this is not intended to be a diet book, though it can easily become one either by eliminating one of the dishes on a menu or, better yet, by eating everything on the menu in smaller quantities. On the other hand, you may want to keep your weight just as it is, or even not object to gaining a pound or so. The answer is obvious. Lucky you, who can enjoy an extra dessert or an extra indulgence here or there.

My whole approach to slimming and staying slim is to eliminate cravings before they occur. The first question I ask a would-be dieter is "What is your favorite food?" And to the answer I respond that the favorite food will be on the first day's menu and from time to time thereafter. No craving must reach the stage where it is insurmountable. There are few people who can eternally resist all temptation, and hardly any who haven't expressed the thought that if they could just have an occasional piece of bread or a wedge of pie, or whatever type of food they most delight in, they would adhere to the diet happily.

Generally, people fall into one of three classes: those who prefer sweets, starches, or proteins. To court the favor of "sweet" lovers, to win the approval of "starch" addicts, and to tempt the hearty meat eater, I have devised three basic menus: SWEET menus, STARCH menus, and PROTEIN menus. This means that the emphasis in a SWEET menu, for instance, is on sweets. The emphasis in a STARCH menu is on starchy dishes, and the emphasis on the PROTEIN menus is on proteins. Though the emphasis in each menu is indicated by the category it is placed in, this *does not* mean that a SWEET menu is made up exclusively of "sweet" dishes, a starch menu of only starchy dishes, and so on.

Here is a typical SWEET menu:
Fringed Celery
Roast Leg of Lamb with Mint Jelly
Eggplant Normande
Chocolate Fruit Fondu

Obviously, everything on that menu is not sweet. Furthermore, there is no restriction on switching menus or recipes, as long as the number of calories involved is about the same. For instance, should the SWEET afficionado so desire, he can substitute a PROTEIN or STARCH menu, in part or whole, for a menu or recipe from the SWEET section, assuming always that the caloric count is about the same. He might alter the SWEET menu above by substituting Janet Rather's Zucchini Bake (from the protein dinners) for the Eggplant Normande. Or, he might prefer White Chiffon Layer Cake (from the starch dinners) for the Chocolate Fruit Fondu. Or, he might make *both* changes. Still again, he could elect to substitute completely for the dinner above, by choosing the PROTEIN dinner that features Fillet of Beef Bordelaise. No need to adhere to any single category. Mix them as you will, and budget your calories where they please you most. Allow discreet indulgence in the foods you most enjoy. My menus are only a framework to which you can add embellishments, or delete one dish, or substitute from another menu as long as the dishes are of comparable caloric value. Approximate values are indicated with all of the recipes requiring food preparation. Caloric counts cannot be exact due to the variation in size of an ingredient or a portion. How large, for example, is a "large" apple? How big is an "average" portion? Go right ahead, should you want to substitute a plain roast or a plain vegetable or fruit, let us say, for a prepared dish. The calorie tables in the book will help you effect the switch. You will meet disbelief from people who question the appearance of cream or butter and so forth on a low-calorie menu. Nor can many people understand that 100 calories of whipped cream are no more fattening than 100 calories of tomatoes, or 100 calories of scrambled eggs. Everything is fattening to a degree.

There is more to watching your weight than menus and recipes. Forewarned with the knowledge that embarking on a low-calorie regime is not always a breeze, there are tips and tricks that are helpful. Choose a time to begin when you are relaxed, never a time of tension when food can be an excellent solace. Learn to eat slow-motion. Sip, don't gulp. You will see that it takes less food to satisfy your appetite. Cultivate the gentle art of conversation at the dinner table. Good conversation can help you stretch the dinner hour very pleasantly. Serve foods that take time to eat. Offer a treat, like nuts, but serve them unshelled. The same holds for shrimp or lobster. A novel help is to cook or bake (the richer the better), and give it away. You will enjoy the goodies vicariously and your neighbors will be delighted. And what you don't eat won't make you fat!

I consider the cocktail interval to be the most dangerous time of day in your own home or out at a party. At home, serve Harmless Nibbles (see Index), to which you can help yourself freely. And when you are the guest, you may indulge in something on the Special Treats list (see Index). A bit more caloric, true, but not too devastating. If I know that the party I am going to will be for late dinner, I may fortify myself from either list before I go out. If liquor is consumed, make it whiskey rather than a mixed drink. The mixed drink will have added calories.

I still love to eat, enjoy cooking and adore parties, those I give and those I go to—as long as my hostess gowns and party dresses remain size twelve.

ELAINE ROSS

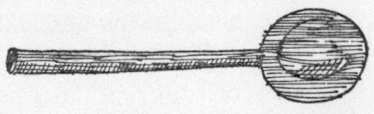

PROTEIN DIET BREAKFASTS

All the breakfast menus total approximately 125 to 185 calories. Feel free to juggle things around a bit. Instead of a poached egg, scramble an egg in a nonstick pan, or make a small omelette—plain or *fines herbes*. Instead of sliced prosciutto, you may have bacon, providing it is crisp. (The more fat you can drain off, the fewer calories are left in the bacon.)

Protein Diet Breakfast #1

Bouillon, Hot or Chilled
Poached Egg
Small Slice of Light Rye Bread
Tea or Coffee with Approved Artificial Sweetener and Skim Milk

Protein Diet Breakfast #2

Frosty Tomato Juice with a Wedge of Lemon
Small Scoop of Cottage Cheese
2 Melba Toast Rounds
Tea or Coffee with Approved Artificial Sweetener and Skim Milk

Protein Diet Breakfast #3

2 Slices of Very Ripe Melon (not watermelon)
2 Slices of Prosciutto or Westphalian Ham
1 Thin Breadstick (*grissino* or similar type)
Tea or Coffee with Approved Artificial Sweetener and Skim Milk

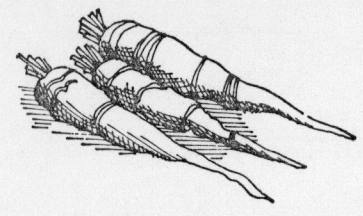

STARCH DIET BREAKFASTS

All the breakfast menus total approximately 125 to 185 calories. To avoid monotony, buy the individual boxes of dry cereal and vary from day to day. Allow one box for each serving and confine your choice to those with lower calorie contents. (The calories are printed on the package.)

Starch Diet Breakfast #1

Individual Box of Rice Krispies with a Little Sugar and Skim Milk
1 Zwieback
Tea or Coffee with Approved Artificial Sweetener and Skim Milk

Starch Diet Breakfast #2

Individual Box of Special K with a Little Sugar and Skim Milk
1 Slice of Crusty Italian or French Bread Lightly Buttered
Tea or Coffee with Approved Artificial Sweetener and Skim Milk

Starch Diet Breakfast #3

Individual Box of Sugar Pops with a Little Skim Milk (Sugar Pops are already sweetened.)
1 Slice of Low-Calorie Bread with a Thin Coating of Jelly or Jam
Tea or Coffee with Approved Artificial Sweetener and Skim Milk

SWEET DIET BREAKFASTS

All the breakfast menus total approximately 125 to 185 calories. Switch one fruit for another, or one juice for another as long as the caloric content is roughly the same. Likewise follow your preference for one sweet biscuit rather than another.

Sweet Diet Breakfast #1

1 slice of Chilled Fresh Pineapple Sprinkled with Minced Fresh Mint
1 Graham Cracker
Tea or Coffee with Approved Artificial Sweetener and Skim Milk

Sweet Diet Breakfast #2

Approximately ½ cup Ripe Strawberries Tossed with 1 tablespoon Defrosted Frozen Raspberries
1 Social Tea Biscuit
Tea or Coffee with Approved Artificial Sweetener and Skim Milk

Sweet Diet Breakfast #3

Orange and Grapefruit Juice Frappé (approximately ⅓ cup each over crushed ice in a large glass)
1 Arrowroot Biscuit
Tea or Coffee with Approved Artificial Sweetener and Skim Milk

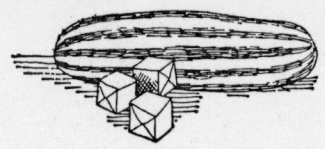

HARMLESS NIBBLES

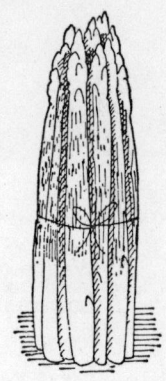

Asparagus
Green beans or wax beans
Broccoli
Cauliflower
Cabbage
Celery
Swiss chard
Cucumber
Kohlrabi
Lettuce
Mushrooms
Green or sweet red pepper
Radishes
Spinach
Summer squash
Watercress
Zucchini

SPECIAL TREATS

Wedge of cantaloupe or honeydew melon
Low-calorie gelatin dessert, as is, or with added fruit
Ice milk
Fresh strawberries, raspberries, blueberries
Fresh pineapple
Citrus fruit
Small pear or peach
Low-calorie matzoth
Scandinavian thin crisp bread
Rye or white Melba toast
Low-calorie bread (½ slice)
Consommé with fine noodles
White meat of chicken or turkey, sliced very thin
Jellied beef or chicken consommé
Celery with prosciutto
Celery filled with a little tartar steak
Mussels, oysters, or clams
Lobster, crab meat, or shrimps
Crab legs or claws

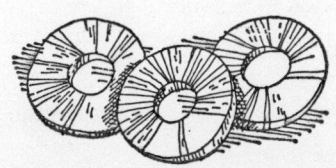

PROTEIN

1 * Endive with Canadian Bacon   18
   Small Melba Toast Rounds
   Grapefruit Sections Marinated in Orange Juice

2 * Tuna Fish Chef's Salad   19
  * Creamy Salad Dressing   19
   2 Low-calorie Matzoth Miniatures

3 * Crab Coquilles   20
  * Carrie Beck's Cucumber Salad   21

4 * Tomato Stuffed with Crabmeat   21
   Watercress Dressed with Lemon Juice
   Triscuit Wafer

5 * Baked Oysters under a Blanket of Cress   22
   Coleslaw
   Sliced Fresh Peach in Season

6 * Scrambled Eggs, Cowboy Style   23
   Garlic-flavored Toast Rounds
   Leaf Lettuce with Low-calorie Italian Dressing

(* indicates recipe is given)

LUNCHES

7 *Last-of-the-Turkey Soup 24
 Carrot Sticks
 Low-calorie Gelatin Dessert

8 *Eggplant Quiche 25
 Asparagus-Tip Salad
 Crenshaw Melon

9 *Cold Fish in Parsley Sauce 27
 Cucumber Sticks
 Fresh Plum or Tangerine

10 *Louisiana Shrimps 28
 *Layered Squash and Poached Egg 28
 Scandinavian Flat Bread

11 *Egg in a Nest 30
 *Ham Rolls Argenteuil 31

12 *Tomato Broth with Peas 32
 *Eggs and Celery Root on a Bed of Shimmering Aspic 33

   (* indicates recipe is given)

1

Endive with Canadian Bacon
Small Melba Toast Rounds
Grapefruit Sections Marinated in Orange Juice
Tea or Coffee with Approved Artificial Sweetener
and Skim Milk

Endive with Canadian Bacon

For each serving:
2 large heads of endive
Dash of grated nutmeg
2 thick julienne strips of Canadian bacon
½ cup well-seasoned chicken stock
Sprinkling of chopped hard-cooked egg

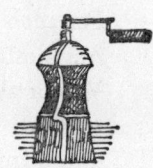

Cut out the root ends of the endive and cut each head almost into halves. Dust lightly with nutmeg, place a strip of Canadian bacon down the slit center of each head, and place the endives side by side in a small shallow baking dish. Pour in the chicken stock, cover the pan completely with a tight-fitting cover or foil, and bake in a preheated 375°F. oven for 40 minutes, or until tender. Remove the foil, raise the heat to 425°F. and bake, basting frequently, until the liquid has almost evaporated. Remove pan from oven and transfer endive to a hot plate. Sprinkle the endive with chopped egg.

SERVES 1 · Approximately 110 to 125 calories each serving

2

Tuna Fish Chef's Salad
Creamy Salad Dressing
2 Low-calorie Matzoth Miniatures
Tea or Coffee with Approved Artificial Sweetener
and Skim Milk

Tuna Fish Chef's Salad

For each serving:
Any desired combination of lettuce, as much as desired
⅓ of a 7½-ounce can of chunk tuna fish, completely drained of oil
3 to 6 fresh mushrooms, sliced thin
⅓ hard-cooked egg, chopped
1 teaspoon drained capers

Wash and dry the lettuce and crisp it in the refrigerator. Break into bite-size pieces and place in a bowl. Crumble the tuna fish into coarse pieces, and scatter them over the lettuce with the remaining ingredients. Chill until serving time. Spoon Creamy Salad Dressing (below) or any prepared low-calorie dressing over the salad, toss, and serve immediately.

SERVES 1 · Approximately 95 to 110 calories each serving

Creamy Salad Dressing

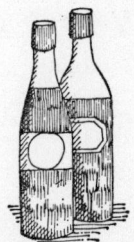

½ cup buttermilk
2 tablespoons small-curd cottage cheese
¼ teaspoon salt
¼ teaspoon coarse black pepper
¼ teaspoon French's mustard

2 scallions, including the green part, sliced
1 tablespoon minced parsley

Put all the ingredients in an electric blender and whirl until smooth. Makes about ⅔ cup dressing.
Approximately 9 to 11 calories per tablespoon

3

Crab Coquilles
Carrie Beck's Cucumber Salad
Tea or Coffee with Approved Artificial Sweetener
and Skim Milk

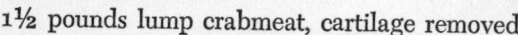

Crab Coquilles

1 egg
3 tablespoons sour cream
1½ tablespoons mayonnaise
2 teaspoons prepared mustard
1 tablespoon minced parsley
1 tablespoon minced chives
Salt
1½ pounds lump crabmeat, cartilage removed

Beat the egg lightly and stir in the sour cream, mayonnaise, mustard, parsley and chives. Add salt to taste. Pour over the crabmeat, toss lightly, and spoon into 6 large clam or scallop shells. Bake in a preheated 400°F. oven for 12 to 15 minutes, or until bubbling.

SERVES 6 · Approximately 150 to 175 calories each serving

Carrie Beck's Cucumber Salad

3 large cucumbers, peeled and sliced thin
1 scant teaspoon salt
3 scallions, including some of the green part, sliced very thin
1 tablespoon oil
1 tablespoon vinegar
1 teaspoon sugar
Dash of white pepper

Place the cucumbers in a bowl. Sprinkle with salt, place a weight on top, and leave for 1 hour. Squeeze out all the liquid, and add the scallions. Combine remaining ingredients in a small saucepan, bring to a boil, and pour over the cucumbers. Chill.

SERVES 6 · Approximately 30 to 35 calories each serving

4

Tomato Stuffed with Crabmeat
Watercress Dressed with Lemon Juice
Triscuit Wafer
Tea or Coffee with Approved Artificial Sweetener
and Skim Milk

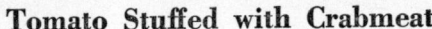

Tomato Stuffed with Crabmeat

1 large tomato
1 teaspoon mayonnaise
1 tablespoon low-calorie sour cream or sour half-and-half
½ teaspoon prepared mustard
1 teaspoon drained capers
1 small water chestnut, diced
¼ pound crabmeat, cartilage removed

Scoop out the tomato, keeping the outside wall intact. Chop and reserve the pulp. Allow the tomato to drain, upside down, until serving time. Meanwhile, prepare the filling: Mix the mayonnaise, sour cream, mustard, capers and water chestnut. At serving time, fold the chopped tomato pulp and the crabmeat into the filling. Set the tomato on a plate, fill with the crabmeat mixture, and serve immediately.

SERVES 1 · Approximately 200 to 215 calories each serving

5

Baked Oysters under a Blanket of Cress
Coleslaw
Sliced Fresh Peach in Season
(Substitute pear or pineapple.)
Tea or Coffee with Approved Artificial Sweetener
and Skim Milk

Baked Oysters under a Blanket of Cress

1 onion, minced
1 tablespoon butter
3 dozen medium-size oysters in shells
1 bunch of watercress
1 tablespoon bacon fat
1 garlic clove, crushed
½ teaspoon crumbled dried thyme
Salt
¼ cup fine dry bread crumbs

In a large heavy skillet, sauté the onion in the butter over low heat, stirring frequently until the onion is golden. Shuck the oysters and reserve the bottom shells. Add the oysters to the onion and sauté them until the edges curl. Do not crowd the skillet or the oysters will steam and overcook. It is wiser to sauté them in 2 batches if necessary. Place 1 sautéed oyster in each bottom shell. Discard the stems of the watercress and chop the leaves into coarse pieces. Add the cress and the bacon fat to the skillet. Cook for 1 minute, stirring constantly. Add the garlic, thyme, and a little salt, and cook for a few seconds longer. Spread a portion of the mixture over each oyster and sprinkle the bread crumbs on top. Chill for 1 hour. Preheat the oven to 400°F. and bake the oysters for 4 to 5 minutes, or until bubbling. Serve immediately.

SERVES 6 · Approximately 165 to 185 calories each serving

6

Scrambled Eggs, Cowboy Style
Garlic-flavored Toast Rounds (3 for each serving)
Leaf Lettuce with Low-calorie Italian Dressing
Tea or Coffee with Approved Artificial Sweetener
and Skim Milk

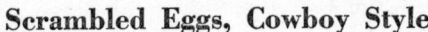

Scrambled Eggs, Cowboy Style

1 slice of lean bacon, diced
1 tablespoon butter
1 cup fine-diced onion
1 cup fine-diced green pepper
¾ pound tomatoes, peeled, seeded, and chopped fine
½ teaspoon sugar
¼ teaspoon crumbled dried thyme
1 garlic clove, mashed
6 eggs
Salt and pepper

In a heavy skillet, over low heat, sauté the bacon in the butter for 5 minutes. Add the onion and pepper and sauté for an additional

10 minutes, or until the onion is translucent. Add the tomatoes, sugar, thyme and garlic, and simmer, uncovered, for 30 minutes, stirring occasionally, until the vegetables are reduced to a thick purée. In another skillet, scramble the eggs in the usual manner. When they are almost set but still moist, add the vegetable purée and salt and pepper to taste. Continue cooking and stirring until set. Serve immediately.

SERVES 6 · Approximately 140 to 160 calories each serving

7

* Last-of-the-Turkey Soup
Carrot Sticks
Low-calorie Gelatin Dessert
Tea or Coffee with Approved Artificial Sweetener
and Skim Milk

Last-of-the-Turkey Soup

Carcass of a cooked turkey
4 cups water
4 cups chicken stock, or 4 chicken bouillon cubes dissolved in 4 cups water
1 slice of lean bacon, minced
1 leek, white part only, trimmed, washed, and sliced
1 tart apple, cored and chopped
1 celery rib, sliced
1 teaspoon curry powder
1 teaspoon salt
1 tablespoon dark brown sugar
1 tablespoon butter
1 tablespoon flour
2 cups diced warm cooked chicken

Break up the turkey carcass and put it into a large pot with the water and chicken stock. Bring the liquid to a boil, skim the surface, reduce the heat and simmer, covered, for 1 hour, or until the liquid has been reduced by one third. If it has not reduced sufficiently, boil it, uncovered, for a few minutes. In a large pan, sauté the bacon with the leek for 3 or 4 minutes, stirring constantly. Add the apple, celery and curry powder to the bacon, and continue stirring for 5 minutes longer. Drain the stock and skim the fat from the surface. Add the stock to the vegetables with the salt and brown sugar and simmer, covered, for 15 minutes. Purée the soup in a blender or in a food mill. In another saucepan melt the butter, stir in the flour, and gradually add the purée. Cook, stirring constantly, until thickened. Taste for salt and add more if necessary. Divide the cooked chicken among 6 soup bowls, pour in the soup, and serve immediately.

SERVES 6 · Approximately 200 to 225 calories each serving

8

Eggplant Quiche
Asparagus-Tip Salad
Crenshaw Melon (or other variety in season)
Tea or Coffee with Approved Artificial Sweetener
and Skim Milk

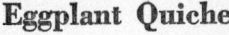

Eggplant Quiche

1 medium-large eggplant
Salt
1½ tablespoons oil
2 ounces Swiss cheese, diced
2 tablespoons flour
1 can (4 ounces) mushroom stems and pieces, drained
1 teaspoon butter

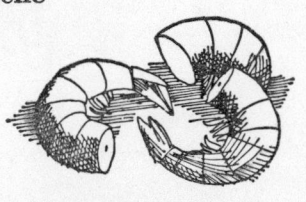

2 tomatoes, sliced thin
15 medium-size shrimps, cooked and cleaned
3 eggs, lightly beaten
1½ cups skim milk
Dash of white pepper
¾ teaspoon salt
Dash of cayenne pepper

Cut the eggplant into slices about ½ inch thick. Sprinkle the slices with salt, let stand for 30 minutes, and pat the eggplant dry. Sauté the slices slowly in the oil in a large heavy skillet until they get flecked with brown and are tender. Line a pie plate (11 to 12 inches) with the eggplant. Mix the Swiss cheese with flour and scatter over the eggplant. Sauté the mushrooms in the butter; scatter them over all. Arrange the tomato slices and shrimps in a pattern on top. Mix the eggs, milk, pepper, salt and cayenne. Pour into the pie plate carefully. Bake in a preheated 400°F. oven for 40 minutes, or until the custard is set.

SERVES 6 · Approximately 180 to 200 calories each serving

9

Cold Fish in Parsley Sauce
Cucumber Sticks
Fresh Plum or Tangerine (depending on the season)
*Tea or Coffee with Approved Artificial Sweetener
and Skim Milk*

Cold Fish in Parsley Sauce

½ cup clam juice
1½ cups water
6 peppercorns
2 bay leaves
2 tablespoons vinegar
1 teaspoon salt
6 fillets of flounder or sole, about 6 ounces each
1 tablespoon butter
3 tablespoons flour
½ cup minced parsley

Combine the clam juice, water, peppercorns, bay leaves, vinegar and salt in a saucepan. Bring to a boil, reduce the heat, cover, and simmer for 10 minutes. Strain the clam stock and set aside. Fold the fillets in half and arrange them in a skillet just large enough to hold the pieces in a single layer. Pour the reserved stock over the fish, cover, and simmer for 10 minutes, or until the fish flakes easily with a fork. Transfer the fish to a serving platter. Strain the cooking liquid and measure 1½ cups.

In a saucepan, melt the butter. Blend in the flour and add the measured stock gradually, stirring until the sauce thickens. Add the parsley, adjust seasonings, and spoon over the fish. Be sure that the sauce is well seasoned; it will become less flavorful as it cools. Chill in the refrigerator.

SERVES 6 · Approximately 235 to 250 calories each serving

10

Louisiana Shrimps
Layered Squash and Poached Egg
Scandinavian Flat Bread
Tea or Coffee with Approved Artificial Sweetener
and Skim Milk

Louisiana Shrimps

1 tablespoon vinegar
2 teaspoons lemon juice
1 tablespoon olive oil
Creole mustard (available in food specialty shops)
Salt
2 scallions, including half of the green part, minced
1 large celery rib, minced
2 tablespoons minced parsley
3 dozen large shrimps, cooked and cleaned (about 1 pound after cleaning)

Combine the vinegar, lemon juice and oil. Add mustard and salt to taste. Combine the scallions, celery and parsley with the shrimps, and toss with the dressing. Refrigerate for several hours.

SERVES 6 · Approximately 160 to 190 calories each serving

Layered Squash and Poached Egg

3 tablespoons oil
5 celery ribs, diced
5 white onions, peeled and diced
2 large tomatoes, peeled and cut into thick slices

1 pound young summer squash, cut into ¼-inch-thick slices
1 pound young zucchini, cut into ¼-inch-thick slices
⅓ cup chicken stock
½ teaspoon salt
4 tablespoons catsup
1 garlic clove, mashed
2 teaspoons Italian seasoning
6 poached eggs (see below)
12 strips of pimiento

Heat a heavy skillet, add 1 tablespoon oil, and sauté the celery and onions, stirring frequently, until almost tender. Spread the vegetables over the bottom of a casserole. Arrange the tomatoes on top. Sauté the summer squash in an additional tablespoon oil until it is almost tender. Spread squash over the tomatoes. Finally, sauté the zucchini in the remaining oil, stirring frequently, until it is almost tender, and spread it on top. Mix the chicken stock, salt, catsup, garlic and Italian seasoning, and pour it over the vegetables. Cover the casserole and bake in a preheated 375°F. oven for 40 minutes, or until tender. If the casserole looks watery, increase the heat to 425°F., uncover the casserole, and bake for 10 minutes longer, or until some of the juices have evaporated. Crisscross 2 strips of pimiento on top of each egg, and arrange the eggs on top of the vegetables. Serve hot or cold.

SERVES 6 · Approximately 195 to 230 calories each serving

Poached Egg

½ teaspoon vinegar
1 egg

Fill a small saucepan with water to a depth of 1 to 1½ inches. Add the vinegar and bring to a slow simmer. Place the egg in its shell in the simmering water for ½ minute, turning it constantly to heat all sides. Remove the egg from the water and break it into a saucer. Bring the saucer close to the water level and tip it quickly so that the egg goes into the water. Let it poach for 3 to 4 minutes before removing with a slotted spoon. Dry on a tea towel. To serve hot, keep in hot water.

11

* *Egg in a Nest*
* *Ham Rolls Argenteuil*
*Tea or Coffee with Approved Artificial Sweetener
and Skim Milk*

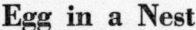

Egg in a Nest

6 medium-large, slightly underripe tomatoes
Salt
1 cup grated Swiss cheese
6 crêpes (see Index, Basic Crêpes)
1½ tablespoons cornstarch
3 eggs, lightly beaten
Coarse-ground black pepper
8 drops of Tabasco

Scald and peel the tomatoes. Cut a slice from the top of each and scoop out the inside, leaving a shell. Sprinkle the interior with salt and turn upside down to drain. Place the top slices and the scooped-out meat in a saucepan. Place over medium heat, mash the tomato with a fork, and cook until it is reduced to a thick purée. Turn the tomato shells right side up, and fill them with grated cheese.

Cut the crêpes into halves. Line 6 buttered custard cups with the halved crêpes. Place 1 tomato in each crêpe-lined cup. Mix the cornstarch, eggs, pepper, Tabasco and tomato purée. Taste for seasoning. Spoon the mixture into the tomato shells, and bake in a preheated 375°F. oven for 25 minutes, or until the custard is set. Serve in the cups, or remove the tomatoes from the cups and place them on individual plates.

SERVES 6 · Approximately 100 to 120 calories each serving

Ham Rolls Argenteuil

Small head of iceberg lettuce, shredded
1 can (15 ounces) green asparagus tips
1 can (15 ounces) white asparagus tips
6 thin slices of boiled ham
Creamy Salad Dressing (see Index)

Arrange the lettuce on a platter or on 6 individual plates. Drain the asparagus tips. Cut the slices of ham into halves. Divide the asparagus into 6 bunches of green tips and 6 bunches of white tips. Enfold each bunch in a slice of ham, allowing the tips to project at one end. Alternate the rolls on the platter, or place one roll of each color on the individual plates. Serve the dressing separately, allowing about 1 tablespoon for each serving.

SERVES 6 · Approximately 225 to 250 calories for each serving

12

* Tomato Broth with Peas
* Eggs and Celery Root on a Bed of Shimmering Aspic
Tea or Coffee with Approved Artificial Sweetener
and Skim Milk

Tomato Broth with Peas

3 cups tomato juice
10 whole allspice berries
2 tablespoons minced onion
1 tablespoon lemon juice
1 tablespoon sugar
Salt and pepper
¼ cup shelled fresh young peas

Place the tomato juice, allspice berries, onion, lemon juice and sugar in a saucepan. Bring to a boil, reduce the heat, and simmer for 5 minutes. Strain the liquid and add salt and pepper to taste. Pour into 6 soup cups and add a few peas to each serving.

SERVES 6 · Approximately 25 to 30 calories each serving

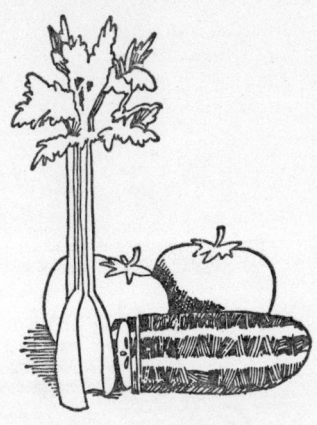

Eggs and Celery Root on a Bed of Shimmering Aspic

1 envelope unflavored gelatin
⅓ cup water
1 can (10½ ounces) beef consommé with added gelatin
6 large slices of canned celery root or the equivalent of freshly cooked (Slices of fresh-cooked celery root are not uniformly large. If necessary, use additional slices.)
9 hard-cooked eggs
1 tablespoon sour cream
3 tablespoons low-calorie Thousand Island dressing

Soak the gelatin in the water, then heat until the gelatin dissolves. Add to the consommé and pour into a round or square pan (8 or 9 inches across) that has been rinsed in cold water. Chill until very firm. Remove the aspic to a board, chop it with a chef's knife, and spoon it over a serving platter. Place the celery root, evenly spaced, on the aspic. Cut the eggs crosswise into halves and place 3 halves, rounded side up, on each slice of celery root. (If you have to use smaller slices of celery root, allow 1 small slice for each hard-cooked egg half.) Mix the sour cream with the Thousand Island dressing and spread a little on each egg.

SERVES 6 · Approximately 165 to 185 calories each serving

STARCH

1 *Custom-made Heroes 36
  Orange Sections with Jam

2 *Mushrooms on Toast Continentale 37
  *Jellied Tomato Mold 38

3 Hot Madrilene
  *Glorified French Loaf 39
  Escarole

4 *Swiss Oatmeal Soup 40
  *Egg Salad Sandwich 41

5 *Spinach Soup with Dumplings 41
  *Muffin Strips 42
  Half Grapefruit

6 *Pasta Shell Soup Renata 43
  *Neapolitan Toasts 44
  Low-calorie Gelatin Dessert

(* indicates recipe is given)

LUNCHES

7 * Bacon and Oatmeal Vegetable Soup 45
  * Chive Fingers 46
    Fresh Pineapple

8 * Jellied Clam Coquilles 46
  * Manicotti Blintzes with Tomato Sauce 47

9 * Palm Beach Conch Chowder 49
  * Cheese and Radish Open Sandwich 50

10 * Salmon Mold 50
   * Baked Potato with Caviar 51

11 * Egg en Gelée with Vermouth 52
   * Sheila Stone's Ratatouille Crêpes 53

12 * Oxtail Soup 54
   * Smoked-Salmon and Mushroom Open Sandwich 55

(* indicates recipe is given)

1

Custom-made Heroes
Orange Sections Topped with a Spoonful of Low-calorie Jam
Tea or Coffee with Approved Artificial Sweetener
and Skim Milk

Custom-made Heroes

1 loaf of French or Italian bread
2 tomatoes, sliced
1 small cucumber, peeled and sliced thin
1 small red onion, peeled and sliced thin
3 hard-cooked eggs, sliced
1 can (7 ounces) chunk-style tuna fish, very well drained
1 can (2 ounces) flat anchovies
1 can (4 ounces) pimientos, very well drained
Small bunch of escarole, washed, drained, and crisped
Any low-calorie Italian salad dressing

Shortly before serving, wrap the bread in foil and heat it. Cut it lengthwise into halves but do not cut all the way through; then cut it crosswise into 6 portions. Arrange all the filling ingredients in small bowls.

Each person makes his own sandwich, we hope, favoring large amounts of vegetable fillings and lesser amounts of high-calorie ingredients. Spoon a bit of the salad dressing over the sandwich ingredients before replacing the top slice of bread.

SERVES 6 · Approximately 150 to 275 calories each serving

2

* *Mushrooms on Toast Continentale*
* *Jellied Tomato Mold*
*Tea or Coffee with Approved Artificial Sweetener
and Skim Milk*

Mushrooms on Toast Continentale

For each serving:
1 can (3½ to 4 ounces) mushrooms (preferably imported from Europe)
1 teaspoon oil
⅛ teaspoon crumbled dried thyme
⅓ teaspoon Italian seasoning
Dash of garlic powder
Grinding of coarse black pepper
1 teaspoon flour
1 teaspoon sour cream
Salt
1 slice of low-calorie bread, toasted
1 teaspoon minced parsley

Drain the mushrooms, reserving the liquid. Heat the oil in a small heavy skillet. Add the mushrooms, thyme, Italian seasoning, garlic powder and pepper to the oil. Cook over high heat, stirring constantly, until almost all the liquid from the mushrooms has evaporated. Measure the reserved liquid and add water if necessary to make ½ cup. Mix the flour with the sour cream and add the mushroom liquid gradually. Pour over the mushrooms and cook, stirring constantly, until the sauce is thickened. Add salt to taste. Place the toast on a plate, pour the mushrooms and sauce over the toast, sprinkle with parsley, and serve immediately.

SERVES 1 · Approximately 110 to 125 calories each serving

Jellied Tomato Mold

For each serving:
½ cup canned Italian plum tomatoes
1 scallion, including some of the green part, sliced
1 small celery rib with leaves, minced
½ teaspoon chili sauce
½ teaspoon brown sugar
¼ teaspoon Italian seasoning
1 drop of Tabasco
Salt and pepper
¾ teaspoon unflavored gelatin
2 lettuce leaves

Mix all the ingredients except the salt and pepper, gelatin and lettuce leaves in a saucepan. Bring to a boil, reduce the heat, cover, and simmer for 20 minutes, or until the vegetables are tender. Purée in an electric blender or a food mill, measure, and if necessary, add water to make ½ cup liquid. Add salt and pepper to taste. Soak the gelatin in 1 tablespoon water, add it to the purée, and heat until the gelatin is dissolved. Pour the mixture into a custard cup or small mold that has been rinsed in cold water. Chill and unmold onto lettuce leaves.

SERVES 1 · Approximately 65 to 85 calories each serving

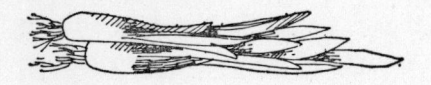

3

Hot Madrilene
*Glorified French Loaf
Escarole (*hearts only, with any low-calorie dressing*)
Tea or Coffee with Approved Artificial Sweetener
and Skim Milk

Glorified French Loaf

2 pieces of French bread, each about 5 inches long and 3 to 3½ inches in diameter
1 large onion, minced
2 teaspoons oil
3 tablespoons drained capers
3 tablespoons minced parsley
1 cup well-packed minced cooked chicken, veal, or seafood
1 egg, lightly beaten
Salt
2 tablespoons butter

Scoop out the inside crumb of the bread, leaving a shell about ½ inch thick. Soak the crumb in water and squeeze dry. In a heavy skillet (preferably one with a nonstick coating) sauté the onion in the oil until golden. Add the capers, parsley, and minced cooked meat or seafood, and cook for a few seconds longer. Remove the pan from the heat and add the egg, soaked bread, and salt to taste; mix well. Spoon the filling into the bread shell. Chill for 1 hour or longer, until the bread is firm enough to slice.

With a serrated knife, cut each piece into 6 equal slices and chill them until serving time. Melt a little of the butter in the skillet and sauté the slices, a few at a time, on both sides. Keep the finished slices hot in a warm oven until all are ready to be served.

SERVES 6 · Approximately 250 to 275 calories each serving

4

Swiss Oatmeal Soup
Egg Salad Sandwich
Tea or Coffee with Approved Artificial Sweetener and Skim Milk

Swiss Oatmeal Soup

1 medium-size onion, peeled and minced
1 tablespoon butter
⅓ cup Scotch or Irish oatmeal
6 cups beef consommé, or 9 beef bouillon cubes dissolved in 6 cups water
2 tablespoons minced parsley
Salt and pepper

In a large saucepan, over medium heat, sauté the onion in the butter until translucent and golden. Add the oatmeal and cook for 2 minutes longer, stirring constantly. Add the beef consommé, reduce the heat and simmer, covered, for 2 hours. If the soup has not thickened to the consistency of a thin cream soup, uncover and reduce rapidly over high heat, stirring frequently. Add the parsley, and salt and pepper to taste.

SERVES 6 · Approximately 55 to 65 calories each serving

Egg Salad Sandwich

For each serving:
1 hard-cooked egg, chopped
Low-calorie Thousand Island or any preferred low-calorie dressing
Lettuce
2 slices of very thin-sliced bread or low-calorie bread

Mix the egg with enough dressing to make the mixture spreadable. Make a sandwich in the usual fashion, using any desired amount of lettuce.

SERVES 1 · Approximately 155 to 165 calories each serving

5

Spinach Soup with Dumplings
Muffin Strips
Half Grapefruit
Tea or Coffee with Approved Artificial Sweetener and Skim Milk

Spinach Soup with Dumplings

1 large onion, minced
1 teaspoon butter
1 quart beef stock
¾ cup old-fashioned oatmeal
¼ cup cracked wheat (fine bulgur)
½ teaspoon salt
⅛ teaspoon coarse black pepper
1 tablespoon catsup

1 teaspoon vinegar
½ package (10 ounces) frozen chopped spinach, defrosted, drained, and pressed dry

In a large saucepan, sauté the onion in the butter until golden, stirring constantly. Add the beef stock and bring to a boil. Mix the oatmeal, cracked wheat, salt and black pepper, add ¼ cup water, and knead until the mixture holds together. Roll into small balls about ¾ inch in diameter. Drop the dumplings into the stock, cover, and simmer over low heat for 20 minutes. Add the catsup, vinegar and spinach, and simmer for 5 minutes longer. Adjust seasonings.

SERVES 6 · Approximately 90 to 110 calories each serving

Muffin Strips

2 large English muffins
4 teaspoons softened butter

Slice the muffins crosswise into strips a scant ¼ inch thick. If they are chilled, they slice more easily. Butter each slice lightly and place on a cooky sheet. Bake in a preheated 350°F. oven for 20 minutes, or until crisp.

MAKES 20 to 24 strips · Approximately 11 to 12 calories each strip

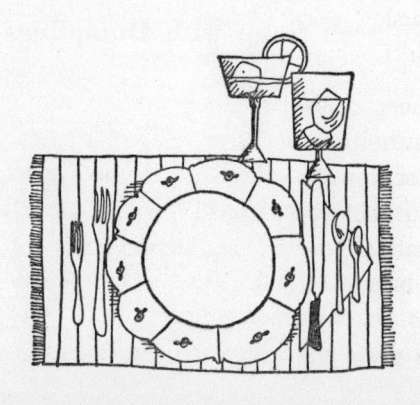

6

Pasta Shell Soup Renata
Neapolitan Toasts
Low-calorie Gelatin Dessert
Tea or Coffee with Approved Artificial Sweetener
and Skim Milk

Pasta Shell Soup Renata

1 large red onion, diced
1 teaspoon oil
3 chicken livers
1½ cups canned Italian plum tomatoes
1 teaspoon dried orégano
1 teaspoon dried basil
½ teaspoon sugar
1½ teaspoons salt
Dash of pepper
1 small garlic clove, mashed
6 chicken bouillon cubes dissolved in 4¼ cups water
¼ pound small pasta shells
¼ cup parsley, stems removed
1 teaspoon Escoffier Sauce Diable

In a large saucepan, over medium heat, sauté the onion in the oil for 5 minutes. Add the livers and sauté them until they lose their pink color. Remove the livers, dice them fine, and reserve. To the onion in the saucepan add the canned tomatoes, orégano, basil, sugar, salt, pepper and garlic. Cook for 1 minute, add the bouillon, and bring to a boil. Reduce the heat, cover, and simmer for 20 minutes.

Cook the pasta shells according to package directions and

drain. Reserve half of the cooked shells. Add the remainder to the broth and vegetables with the parsley and Escoffier Sauce. Purée the mixture, a portion at a time, in an electric blender. Add the reserved diced chicken livers and the reserved cooked pasta shells. Serve piping hot.

SERVES 6 · Approximately 120 to 135 calories each serving

Neapolitan Toasts

6 slices of French or Italian bread, a scant ¼ inch thick
1 to 2 tablespoons low-calorie Italian dressing

Chill or freeze the bread for easier slicing. Spread the slices with Italian dressing, place them on a baking sheet, and bake in a preheated 300°F. oven for 20 minutes, or until crisp and golden.

MAKES 6 slices · Approximately 25 to 27 calories each slice

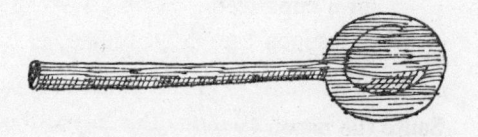

7

* Bacon and Oatmeal Vegetable Soup
* Chive Fingers
Fresh Pineapple
Tea or Coffee with Approved Artificial Sweetener and Skim Milk

Bacon and Oatmeal Vegetable Soup

1 slice of lean bacon, diced
1 small head of cabbage, cored and shredded
2 celery ribs, cut into ½-inch slices
1 white turnip, peeled and cut into bite-size pieces
1 small yellow turnip, peeled and cut into bite-size pieces
1 large carrot, scraped and sliced thin
1 large yellow onion, peeled and diced
1 leek, white part only, cut into ½-inch slices
¼ pound green beans, trimmed and cut into ½-inch slices
¼ pound wax beans, trimmed and cut into ½-inch slices
⅓ cup old-fashioned oatmeal
1 cup canned Italian plum tomatoes, chopped into coarse pieces
1 quart clear beef stock, or 4 beef bouillon cubes dissolved in 4 cups water
⅛ teaspoon coarse black pepper
Salt

Sauté the bacon in a soup kettle until the bacon is crisp. Remove the bacon and reserve. Add the cabbage, celery, white and yellow turnips, carrot, onion, leek, green and wax beans. Cook over low heat, stirring frequently, for 10 minutes. Add the oatmeal, tomatoes and beef stock. Bring to a boil. Reduce the heat and simmer, covered, for 2½ hours, or until the soup is thick. Add the pepper, reserved bacon, and salt to taste. Serve immediately, or reheat to serve.

SERVES 6 · Approximately 120 to 140 calories each serving

Chive Fingers

2 slices of firm-textured oatmeal bread
2 teaspoons salt butter
1 tablespoon minced chives

Trim the crusts from the bread. Spread the slices with butter and sprinkle with chives. Cut each piece into 3 fingers.

MAKES 6 fingers · Approximately 25 calories each finger

8

Jellied Clam Coquilles
Manicotti Blintzes with Tomato Sauce
Tea or Coffee with Approved Artificial Sweetener
and Skim Milk

Jellied Clam Coquilles

1 can (10½ ounces) beef consommé with added gelatin
2 tablespoons chopped onion, fresh or frozen
Small handful of celery leaves
1 thin lemon slice
1 teaspoon unflavored gelatin
2 tablespoons cold water
1 tablespoon dry vermouth
1 can (7½ ounces) minced clams
2 tablespoons minced parsley

Place half of the can of consommé, the onion, celery leaves and lemon slice in a small saucepan. Simmer, covered, for 10 minutes. Soak gelatin in the cold water. Strain the simmered consommé, add the soaked gelatin, and stir till dissolved. Add the remaining half can of the consommé and the vermouth, and place in the freezer for 30 minutes. Add the clams and parsley and refrigerate again for 30 minutes. Stir to distribute the clams and parsley evenly. Chill for about 30 minutes longer, or till set. Spoon into 6 shells or small cups. Refrigerate till serving time.

SERVES 6 · Approximately 30 to 35 calories each serving

Manicotti Blintzes

¾ pound cottage cheese, drained in a sieve
2 tablespoons minced parsley or dried parsley flakes
1 egg yolk
Grated Parmesan cheese (about ½ cup)
Double recipe Basic Crêpes (see Index)
Tomato Sauce (below)
Butter for frying

In an electric mixer, beat the cottage cheese, parsley, egg yolk, and ¼ cup Parmesan cheese until smooth. Place the 12 crêpes, brown side up, on a board or working surface. Divide the cheese filling among the crêpes, placing the filling to one side of each crêpe. Fold the edge of the crêpe over the filling, then fold each side of the crêpe toward the center. Finally, roll the crêpe to enclose the filling completely. Refrigerate until serving time.

Heat the tomato sauce. Melt enough butter to coat the bottom of a heavy skillet lightly. Fry the blintzes on both sides until golden brown. Serve on a platter or on individual plates. Spoon the sauce over the blintzes, or serve the sauce separately. Pass additional Parmesan cheese.

SERVES 6 · Approximately 175 to 190 calories each serving

Tomato Sauce

1 can (1 pound) Italian peeled tomatoes
1 medium-size onion, minced
1 large celery rib with leaves, minced
2 teaspoons catsup
1 teaspoon sugar
1 teaspoon Italian seasoning
1 teaspoon salt
Generous grinding of black pepper
4 drops of Tabasco

Drain the liquid from the tomatoes into a saucepan. Chop the tomatoes and add to the juice in the saucepan with all the other ingredients. Bring to a boil, reduce the heat, cover, and simmer for 20 minutes, or until the vegetables are tender. Purée half of the mixture in an electric blender or in a food mill; combine with the remaining sauce. Taste, and add more seasoning if necessary.

MAKES approximately 2 cups sauce

9

* *Palm Beach Conch Chowder*
* *Cheese and Radish Open Sandwich*
*Tea or Coffee with Approved Artificial Sweetener
and Skim Milk*

Palm Beach Conch Chowder

1½ pounds conch meat
1 green pepper, seeded and diced
1 medium-size onion, peeled and diced
1 large potato, peeled and diced
3 celery ribs, cut into 1-inch pieces
1 slice of bacon, diced fine
1 large tomato, peeled, seeded, and diced
1 teaspoon Escoffier Sauce Diable
1 garlic clove, crushed
1 teaspoon salt
¼ teaspoon crumbled dried thyme
⅛ teaspoon coarse black pepper
2 tablespoons dry sherry

Cook the conch in boiling salted water to cover for 30 minutes. Reserve the stock and add water to make 3 cups. Grind the conch meat with the pepper, onion, potato and celery, using the finest blade of a food grinder.

In a large heavy saucepan, sauté the bacon until brown. Add the ground conch and vegetables. Cook, stirring constantly, for 5 minutes. Add the tomato, Escoffier Sauce, garlic, salt, thyme, black pepper, and reserved stock. Bring to a boil, reduce the heat and simmer, covered, for 1 hour, stirring occasionally. Adjust seasonings. At serving time, heat thoroughly and add the sherry.

SERVES 6 · Approximately 150 to 175 calories each serving

Cheese and Radish Open Sandwich

For each serving:
1 large slice of seeded rye bread
2 tablespoons small-curd cottage cheese, as dry as possible
Radishes
¼ teaspoon caraway seeds

With a glass or cooky cutter, cut as large a circle as possible from the rye bread. Mash the cheese with a fork, and spread it evenly on the bread. Cut enough paper-thin radish slices to place them, slightly overlapping, around the edge of the sandwich. Sprinkle the caraway seeds on top.

SERVES 1 • Approximately 80 to 90 calories each serving

10

Salmon Mold
Baked Potato with Caviar
Tea or Coffee with Approved Artificial Sweetener
and Skim Milk

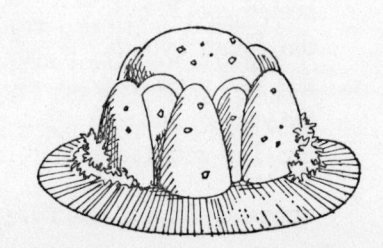

~~~~~

Salmon Mold

1 pound canned salmon
1 envelope unflavored gelatin
¼ cup cold water
1 egg, beaten
1 teaspoon prepared mustard
½ teaspoon salt
1½ tablespoons sugar
Dash of white pepper

¼ cup vinegar
1 cup skim milk
2 large heads of endive, sliced

Place the salmon in a colander, pour boiling water over it, and drain. Remove the skin and bones and flake the fish. Soak the gelatin in the cold water. In a saucepan, mix the egg, mustard, salt, sugar, pepper and vinegar. Add the skim milk and cook over very low heat, stirring constantly, until the custard coats the spoon. Remove from the heat, add the gelatin, and stir till dissolved. Add the flaked salmon. Pour into a 4-cup ring mold or fish mold that has been rinsed with cold water. Chill until set.

Run the tip of a small sharp knife around the inside of the mold, hold the bottom of the mold in hot water for a few seconds, and unmold onto a serving platter on which you have arranged a bed of sliced endive.

SERVES 6 · Approximately 115 to 125 calories each serving

Baked Potato with Caviar

For each serving:
1 medium-size baking potato (preferably Idaho potato)
2 teaspoons cottage cheese
2 teaspoons yoghurt
2 teaspoons sour cream
1 small scallion, white part only, sliced thin
1 teaspoon caviar (preferably black Beluga caviar)

Make a small incision in the top of the potato and bake it in a preheated 400°F. oven for 45 minutes, or until soft. Make a slit in the potato by extending the small incision almost from end to end, and press it open a little. Mash the cottage cheese, mix with the yoghurt and sour cream, and spoon the mixture into the opening. Top with the scallion and caviar.

SERVES 1 · Approximately 150 to 165 calories each serving

11

* Egg en Gelée with Vermouth
* Sheila Stone's Ratatouille Crêpes
Tea or Coffee with Approved Artificial Sweetener
and Skim Milk

Egg en Gelée with Vermouth

- 2 envelopes unflavored gelatin
- ½ cup water
- 2 cans (10½ ounces each) beef consommé with added gelatin
- 2 tablespoons dry vermouth
- 6 eggs
- 4 teaspoons sour cream
- 4 teaspoons minced parsley

Soak the gelatin in the cold water for 3 minutes and dissolve over low heat. Add the consommé and the vermouth. Pour a ⅓-inch-thick layer of liquid aspic into 6 custard cups or 6-ounce ramekins that have been rinsed in cold water. Chill in the freezer for a few minutes, or until set. Do *not* allow them to freeze.

Meanwhile, cook the eggs in their shells for 6 minutes, peel them carefully, and chill them. Place 1 egg in each cup, and fill the cup with the remaining aspic. Chill until set.

With a small sharp knife, loosen the molds from the sides of the cups and hold each cup in hot water for a few seconds to loosen the bottom. Turn out onto 6 individual plates. Put a dab of sour cream on top of each mold and sprinkle with parsley.

SERVES 6 · Approximately 110 to 112 calories each serving

Sheila Stone's Ratatouille Crêpes

Double recipe for Basic Crêpes (see Index)
1 green pepper, seeded and cut into julienne strips
1 small eggplant, peeled and cut into ¾-inch cubes
2 medium-size zucchini, cut into ⅛-inch-thick slices
Salt and pepper
2 tablespoons olive oil (This is less than the original amount, but will do well.)
3 medium-size onions, chopped
2 garlic cloves, mashed
2 cans (1 pound each) whole peeled tomatoes, chopped into coarse pieces
Freshly grated Parmesan cheese
3 tablespoons minced parsley

Fry 12 crêpes or as many more as the batter will yield. Cover them until needed. Place the green pepper, eggplant and zucchini in a bowl, sprinkle with 1 teaspoon salt, and leave for 1 hour. Drain off any juices that may have accumulated. Heat the oil in a heavy skillet, brown the drained vegetables lightly, and remove them to a bowl. Add a bit more oil if necessary and sauté the onions over fairly low heat until tender but not brown. Add the garlic and tomatoes, cook together for 3 minutes, and add salt and pepper to taste. Pour off half of the mixture and reserve. Combine the remaining tomato-onion mixture, the reserved browned vegetables, Parmesan cheese to taste, and the parsley in a large heavy saucepan or Dutch oven. Cover and simmer this ratatouille over low heat for an additional 15 minutes, stirring occasionally.

Spread the crêpes, speckled side up, on a board or working surface. Place a portion of ratatouille on the center of each crêpe, roll up the crêpes, and place them, seam side down and in a single layer, in a shallow baking dish that can come to the table. Shortly before serving time, heat the filled crêpes in a preheated

375°F. oven for 15 to 20 minutes. Purée and reheat the reserved tomato-onion mixture and serve as a sauce.

SERVES 6 · Approximately 185 to 210 calories each serving

12

* *Oxtail Soup*
* *Smoked-Salmon and Mushroom Open Sandwich*
Tea or Coffee with Approved Artificial Sweetener and Skim Milk

Oxtail Soup

2 tablespoons butter
1 large carrot, peeled and sliced
1 small turnip, peeled and diced
1 large onion, peeled and diced
1 celery rib, sliced
1 large leek, white part only, sliced thin
1 pound oxtail, cut into pieces
1 veal knuckle, cracked
6 cups beef stock
2 tablespoons flour
3 tablespoons catsup
2 tablespoons dry sherry
Salt and pepper

Melt half of the butter in a Dutch oven. Add the carrot, turnip, onion, celery, leek and oxtail. Sauté, stirring constantly, until the oxtail and vegetables start to take on a little color. Add the veal knuckle and beef stock, bring to a boil, and skim the top. Reduce the heat and simmer, covered, for 3 hours. Discard the veal knuckle. Strain the soup; reserve the oxtail and vegetables. Chill the stock until the fat rises to the top and solidifies. Remove the fat.

Melt the remaining butter in the Dutch oven, blend in the flour, and add the stock gradually, stirring constantly, until the soup thickens. Add the catsup and sherry and simmer for 5 minutes. Return the reserved oxtail and vegetables, heat together for 5 minutes longer, and add salt and pepper to taste. Serve piping hot.

SERVES 6 · Approximately 140 to 185 calories each serving

Smoked-Salmon and Mushroom Open Sandwich

For each serving:
1 slice of low-calorie brown bread
½ teaspoon butter
1 small slice of smoked salmon
2 medium-size mushroom caps
½ tablespoon low-calorie salad dressing
1 lemon slice
1 tiny leaf of Bibb or Boston lettuce
½ teaspoon drained capers

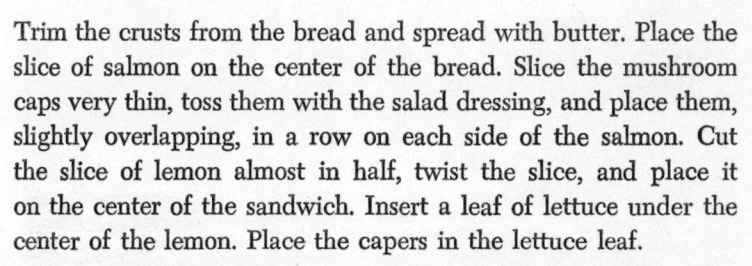

Trim the crusts from the bread and spread with butter. Place the slice of salmon on the center of the bread. Slice the mushroom caps very thin, toss them with the salad dressing, and place them, slightly overlapping, in a row on each side of the salmon. Cut the slice of lemon almost in half, twist the slice, and place it on the center of the sandwich. Insert a leaf of lettuce under the center of the lemon. Place the capers in the lettuce leaf.

SERVES 1 · Approximately 105 to 115 calories each serving

SWEET

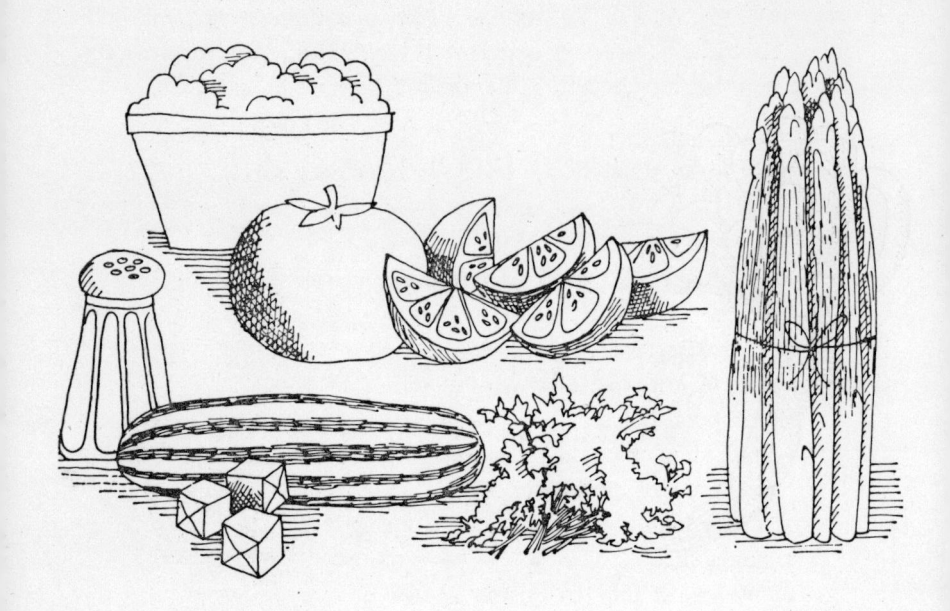

1 * Liptauer Tomato 58
  * Melon Mold with Melon Balls 59
    Wheat Thins

2 * Creamless Cream of Cucumber 59
  * Jelly Omelet 60
    Whole-wheat Melbas

3 * Tomato Bisque on the Rocks 61
  * Fruit and Vegetable Mold 61
    Scandinavian Flat Bread

4 * Stuffed Scampi with Dijon Mustard Sauce 62
    Cold Celery Root
  * Melon Ring with Strawberries 63

5 * Coquille of Halibut and Scallops 64
    Watercress
  * Cottage-Cheese Watermelon Molds 65

6 * Smoked Salmon and Fresh Asparagus 66
  * Chilled Orange Slices with Pistachios 66

   (* indicates recipe is given)

LUNCHES

7 *Mussel Stew   67
   Italian Bread
 *Italian Orange Salad   68

8 Cranberry Juice on the Rocks with a Wedge of Fresh Lime
 *Cantaloupe Dolma   69

9 *Shrimps in a Grapefruit Bowl   70
   Whole-grain Bread with Butter or Jam
   Spoonful of Cottage Cheese

10 Chilled Cauliflower
  *Brochette of Chicken Livers   71
   Applesauce

11 *Bratwurst Soup   72
   Peach Cup

12 *Onion Soup with Poached Egg Oporto   73
  *Fruited Gelatin with Vanilla Cream   74

(* indicates recipe is given)

1

Liptauer Tomato
Melon Mold with Melon Balls
Wheat Thins
Tea or Coffee with Approved Artificial Sweetener
and Skim Milk

Liptauer Tomato

For each serving:
1 large tomato
¼ cup cottage cheese
½ teaspoon prepared mustard, German mustard preferred
½ teaspoon paprika, Hungarian paprika preferred
½ teaspoon sardellen or anchovy paste
½ teaspoon drained capers
3 leaves of lettuce

Scald the tomato in boiling water for a few seconds. Peel it, cut out the stem end, and cut the tomato crosswise into halves. Blend the cottage cheese, mustard, paprika and sardellen paste, and sandwich the mixture between the tomato halves. Put the capers on the stem end of the tomato and set it on a bed of lettuce.

SERVES 1 · Approximately 100 to 110 calories each serving

Melon Molds with Melon Balls

1 large honeydew melon or 2 cantaloupes
2 envelopes (4 servings each) low-calorie orange-flavored gelatin dessert
1 large orange

Make 3 cups of melon balls and chill them. Scoop out all the scraps of melon and purée in an electric blender. Add water, if necessary, to measure 4 cups of liquid in all. Heat the mixture, add the gelatin, and stir until dissolved. Pour into 6 custard cups or molds that have been rinsed in cold water, and chill until firm.

Peel the orange, discard the end slices, and cut the remainder into 6 thin slices. Dip the bottoms of the molds into hot water for a few seconds, and loosen the gelatin from the molds with a small sharp knife. Turn out onto individual dessert plates, place a slice of orange on top of each mold, and spoon the chilled melon balls over all.

SERVES 6 · Approximately 110 to 125 calories each serving

2

Creamless Cream of Cucumber
Jelly Omelet
Whole-wheat Melbas
Tea or Coffee with Approved Artificial Sweetener and Skim Milk

Creamless Cream of Cucumber

1 onion, chopped
2 teaspoons oil
2 medium-size cucumbers, peeled, seeded, and diced

4 chicken bouillon cubes dissolved in 2½ cups water
1 tablespoon minced fresh thyme, or ½ teaspoon dried thyme
1½ tablespoons lemon juice
1 teaspoon sugar
⅓ cup skim milk
⅓ cup yoghurt
Salt and pepper
1 tablespoon minced parsley

Sauté the onion in the oil for 5 minutes. Add the cucumbers and cook for 5 minutes longer. Add the chicken bouillon, thyme, lemon juice and sugar, and bring to a boil. Reduce the heat to medium, cover, and cook for 20 minutes, or until the vegetables are very tender. Cool for a few minutes, then purée a portion at a time in an electric blender. Add the milk and yoghurt, and salt and pepper to taste. Chill and serve cold. Sprinkle some parsley on each portion at serving time.

SERVES 6 · Approximately 25 to 35 calories each serving

Jelly Omelet

For each serving:
2 eggs
1 teaspoon water
Butter
Low-calorie jelly or jam

In a bowl, beat the eggs with the water until well blended but not frothy. Over medium heat, heat an omelet pan or other skillet, preferably a nonstick pan. Take a bit of butter on the end of a fork and coat the surface of the pan lightly with butter. Pour in the beaten eggs. With the flat of the fork, stir the eggs rapidly, meanwhile shaking the pan back and forth with the left hand to keep the omelet loose. When the eggs are set on the bottom but still creamy on top, roll the omelet and tip out onto a plate. Top with a spoonful or two of low-calorie jelly or jam.

SERVES 1 · Approximately 160 to 165 calories each serving

3

Tomato Bisque on the Rocks
Fruit and Vegetable Mold
Scandinavian Flat Bread
Tea or Coffee with Approved Artificial Sweetener
and Skim Milk

Tomato Bisque on the Rocks

2½ cups mixed vegetable juice with tomato
1½ cups buttermilk
6 drops of Tabasco or other hot sauce
1 tablespoon orange juice
1 teaspoon Worcestershire sauce
1½ teaspoons grated orange rind

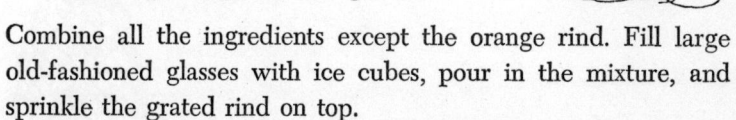

Combine all the ingredients except the orange rind. Fill large old-fashioned glasses with ice cubes, pour in the mixture, and sprinkle the grated rind on top.

SERVES 6 · Approximately 55 to 65 calories each serving

Fruit and Vegetable Mold

1 can (14 ounces) unsweetened sliced pineapple
2 tablespoons orange juice
2 envelopes (4 servings each) low-calorie orange-flavored gelatin dessert

2 or 3 young summer squash, 4 to 5 inches long
1 cup coarse-grated raw carrot
1 teaspoon grated orange rind

Drain the pineapple and reserve the juice. Dice the pineapple and set aside. Combine the reserved juice, orange juice, and enough water to measure 3¼ cups liquid. Heat the liquid, add the gelatin, stir until dissolved, and chill until somewhat thick. Cut off the stems of the squash and cut them lengthwise into halves. Remove the seeds and grate the squash, using the coarse side of the grater. Measure 1 cup of well-packed squash. If necessary, use more squash. Stir the squash, carrot, pineapple and orange rind into the gelatin mixture. Chill in 6 individual molds, or 1 large mold, that have been rinsed in cold water. Turn out onto 6 individual plates or a serving platter.

SERVES 6 · Approximately 75 to 85 calories each serving

4

Stuffed Scampi with Dijon Mustard Sauce
Cold Celery Root
Melon Ring with Strawberries
*Tea or Coffee with Approved Artificial Sweetener
and Skim Milk*

Stuffed Scampi with Dijon Mustard Sauce

24 large shrimps, peeled and deveined
¼ cup minced Canadian bacon
2 tablespoons minced scallions
1 tablespoon fine dry bread crumbs
1 egg yolk

Split the raw shrimps down the back almost through. Rinse them and pat them dry. Mix the remaining ingredients and place a portion on each shrimp. Fold each shrimp to enclose the stuffing and secure with a food pick. Place the shrimps on a rack over boiling water in a shallow pan. Cover the pan and steam the shrimps over simmering water for 8 to 10 minutes, or until pink. Remove the food picks from the shrimps and place the shrimps on a serving platter or on 6 individual plates. Serve the mustard sauce separately.

Dijon Mustard Sauce

1 tablespoon minced scallions
2 teaspoons butter
1½ tablespoons flour
¾ cup skim milk
½ cup dry wine
2 teaspoons Dijon white-wine mustard
1 teaspoon catsup
Salt and white pepper

In a small heavy saucepan, sauté the scallions in the butter until they are translucent. Blend in the flour, cook for 1 minute, gradually add the skim milk and cook, stirring constantly, until the sauce is thick. Stir in the wine, mustard and catsup, and cook over high heat, stirring occasionally, until the sauce is reduced by half. Add salt and pepper to taste.

SERVES 6 · Approximately 175 to 200 calories each serving

Melon Ring with Strawberries

2 packages (4 servings each) low-calorie strawberry-flavored gelatin dessert
⅔ cup hot water
½ cup cold water
2 tablespoons lemon juice
1⅓ cups domestic sauterne
2 cups melon balls (honeydew, Crenshaw, or other melon)
1 pint strawberries
1 tablespoon kirsch

Dissolve the gelatin dessert in the hot water, stirring constantly to break up the lumps. Add the cold water, lemon juice and sauterne. Rinse a 4-cup ring mold with cold water. Spoon the melon balls into the ring, pour in the liquid, and chill until firm.

Run the tip of a small sharp knife around the sides of the mold, dip the bottom of the mold into hot water for a few seconds, and unmold onto a serving platter. Toss the strawberries with the kirsch and spoon into the center of the ring.

SERVES 6 · Approximately 90 to 110 calories each serving

5

Coquille of Halibut and Scallops
Watercress
Cottage-Cheese Watermelon Molds
Tea or Coffee with Approved Artificial Sweetener
and Skim Milk

Coquille of Halibut and Scallops

¾ pound halibut, poached and cooled
¾ pound bay scallops, poached and cooled
1 small onion, minced
1 tablespoon butter
1 egg, lightly beaten
⅔ cup sour cream
½ teaspoon anchovy paste
1 tablespoon minced chives
Salt
2 tablespoons fine dry bread crumbs

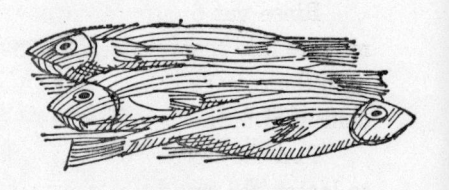

Remove the skin and bones of the halibut, and flake the fish. Mix with the scallops. (If you use sea scallops, cut them into halves; if they are very large, cut them into thirds instead of halves.) Sauté the onion in half of the butter until golden. Remove from the heat. Beat the egg into the sour cream; add the anchovy paste and the chives. Mix with the halibut, scallops and sautéed onion, add salt to taste, and heap in 6 coquilles or small individual baking dishes. Melt the remaining butter, mix with the bread crumbs, and sprinkle over the seafood mixture. Bake in a preheated 425°F. oven for 12 to 15 minutes, or until piping hot.

SERVES 6 · Approximately 190 to 210 calories each serving

Cottage-Cheese Watermelon Molds

Seeded ripe watermelon
1 tablespoon lemon juice
1 envelope unflavored gelatin
1 envelope (4 servings) low-calorie strawberry-flavored gelatin dessert
¾ pound cottage cheese
6 large unhulled strawberries

Using a blender, purée enough watermelon to make 3 cups. Add the lemon juice. Pour the mixture into a saucepan, sprinkle the unflavored gelatin over it, and let it soften for a few minutes. Heat the mixture over medium heat until the gelatin dissolves. Remove from the heat and stir in the strawberry-flavored gelatin dessert. Keep stirring until the gelatin is dissolved and there are no lumps.

Rinse out 6 custard cups with cold water. Pour half of the mixture into them and chill until set. Blend the remaining purée with the cottage cheese in the blender. Pour it into the cups and chill until firm.

Run the tip of a sharp knife around the inside of the molds to loosen the puddings, dip the molds into hot water for a few seconds, and turn the puddings onto individual plates. Place a strawberry on top of each mold.

SERVES 6 · Approximately 115 to 125 calories each serving

6

* Smoked Salmon and Fresh Asparagus
* Chilled Orange Slices with Pistachios
*Tea or Coffee with Approved Artificial Sweetener
and Skim Milk*

Smoked Salmon and Fresh Asparagus

For each serving:
6 large fresh asparagus stalks
3 thin slices of smoked salmon (preferably not salty)
1 teaspoon minced parsley
Coarse black pepper, optional
Wedge of lemon

Peel the asparagus and cook them until just tender. Drain well and arrange on a dinner plate. Lay the slices of salmon, slightly overlapping, on the middle of the asparagus, and sprinkle with parsley. Serve with the peppermill and lemon wedge. The combination of hot asparagus and chilled salmon is different and delicious.

SERVES 1 · Approximately 155 to 175 calories each serving

Chilled Orange Slices with Pistachios

3 medium-size oranges
¼ cup sugar
¼ cup water
1 medium-size banana, sliced thin just before serving time
2 tablespoons minced pistachios

Peel the zest of one of the oranges and set aside. Peel the pith of that orange and peel the other two oranges. Combine the sugar and water in a small saucepan and heat, stirring constantly, until the sugar dissolves. Slice the reserved zest into the thinnest possible julienne strips, add to the saucepan, and cook until the liquid is a light syrup. Slice the oranges thin, discard the end slices, and strain the syrup over the fruit. Reserve the cooked zest. Chill for an hour or more. Arrange the slices slightly overlapping on 6 individual dessert plates. Lift them out of the syrup as you transfer them. You will not want any more syrup than necessary. Place several slices of banana on top and garnish with pistachios and the reserved zest.

SERVES 6 · Approximately 100 to 110 calories each serving

7

Mussel Stew
Italian Bread (1 small slice for each person)
Italian Orange Salad
Tea or Coffee with Approved Artificial Sweetener and Skim Milk

Mussel Stew

- 1 cup minced onions
- 1 tablespoon vegetable oil (not olive oil)
- 2 large tomatoes, peeled, and chopped into coarse pieces
- 1 cup chicken stock, or 1 chicken bouillon cube dissolved in 1 cup water
- ½ cup water
- 1 garlic clove, crushed
- 1 teaspoon dried basil
- 1 tablespoon minced anchovy

4 pounds mussels in the shells
⅔ cup dry white wine (a light wine is preferable)
Salt and pepper
3 tablespoons minced parsley

Sauté the onions in the oil until they are translucent. Add the tomatoes, chicken stock, water, garlic, basil and anchovy; simmer, covered, for 30 minutes. Meanwhile, scrub the mussels to remove as much of the beard as possible. Put them into a large pot, add the wine and cook, covered, over high heat, shaking the pan occasionally, for 7 minutes, or until the shells are open. Discard any that do not open. Remove the mussels from their shells, strain the juice through a cloth-lined sieve, and add to the stew. Add the mussels and salt and pepper to taste. Heat thoroughly and pour into a soup tureen. Sprinkle the parsley on top and serve immediately.

SERVES 6 · Approximately 165 to 185 calories each serving

Italian Orange Salad

For each serving:
1 small white onion, sliced thin
1 teaspoon vinegar
1 tablespoon olive oil
Dash of salt
1 medium-size table orange
1 Italian ripe olive
2 or 3 endive leaves

Place the onion in a small bowl. Mix the vinegar, oil and salt, pour over the onion, and marinate for a few minutes. Peel the orange, making sure to remove all the white pith. Slice the orange thin, discard all the pits, and arrange on a salad plate. Drain the onion thoroughly and place over the orange. Top with the olive and tuck the endive into one side.

SERVES 1 · Approximately 150 to 175 calories

8

Cranberry Juice on the Rocks with a Wedge of Fresh Lime
(Use artificially sweetened juice.)
* Cantaloupe Dolma
Tea or Coffee with Approved Artificial Sweetener
and Skim Milk

Cantaloupe Dolma

3 small cantaloupes
1 large onion, minced
½ tablespoon butter
½ pound lean beef, chopped
1½ cups cooked rice
⅓ teaspoon ground cinnamon
1 teaspoon salt
2 tablespoons dried currants
¼ cup pine nuts

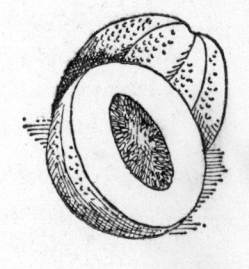

Cut the melons into halves, scoop out the seeds, and let the melons drain upside down. In a heavy skillet sauté the onion in the butter until golden and translucent. Add the beef and cook, stirring constantly, until the meat has lost its red color. Add the rice, cinnamon, salt, currants and pine nuts. Cook for 1 minute and remove from the heat. Turn the melons right side up and fill them with the rice mixture. Wrap each filled melon half in foil, place on a baking sheet, and bake in a preheated 350°F. oven for 1½ hours. Unwrap and serve.

SERVES 6 · Approximately 200 to 220 calories each serving

9

*Shrimps in a Grapefruit Bowl
Whole-grain Bread (1 thin slice lightly spread with butter or jam)
Spoonful of Cottage Cheese
Tea or Coffee with Approved Artificial Sweetener and Skim Milk

Shrimps in a Grapefruit Bowl

3 large grapefruit, cut into halves
Approximately 36 large shrimps, cooked and cleaned
3 tablespoons low-calorie pineapple jam
Low-calorie Thousand Island dressing, optional

Loosen the grapefruit segments, remove every other one and set aside. (If desired, serrate the edges of the grapefruit with a small sharp knife or a pinking shears.) Cut out and discard the cores of the grapefruit and spoon out any excess juice. (Use in some other dish.) Place a shrimp in each of the empty sections, and pile the reserved segments in the center. Top with pineapple jam.

If you wish, serve a low-calorie Thousand Island dressing separately.

SERVES 6 · Approximately 190 to 210 calories each serving

10

Chilled Cauliflower (flowerets, raw or cooked, with low-calorie dressing as dip)
* Brochette of Chicken Livers
Applesauce (preferably unsweetened)
Tea or Coffee with Approved Artificial Sweetener and Skim Milk

Brochette of Chicken Livers

For 1 serving:
1 teaspoon soy sauce
1 teaspoon salad oil
¼ teaspoon garlic powder
3 medium-large firm mushrooms
2 chicken livers
2 large shrimps, cleaned and deveined
¼ teaspoon salt
Dash of white pepper

Mix the soy sauce, salad oil and garlic powder. Brush the mushrooms, livers and shrimps with the mixture and thread them on a skewer, starting and ending with a mushroom, and alternating the livers and shrimps. Do not push the ingredients too close together or they will not have space to cook properly. Sprinkle with salt and pepper. Grill over hot coals or broil about 3 inches from the source of heat, allowing 2 to 3 minutes on each side, or until the livers feel firm to the touch.

SERVES 1 · Approximately 120 to 130 calories each serving

11

Bratwurst Soup
Peach Cup (*halved, pitted, and peeled peach in a wine or champagne glass. Pour in chilled low-calorie cranberry juice or lemon drink shortly before serving time.*)
Tea or Coffee with Approved Artificial Sweetener and Skim Milk

Bratwurst Soup

3 veal bratwurst (or veal and pork bratwurst)
2 teaspoons bacon fat
1 medium-size red onion, chopped
6 very young zucchini, trimmed and cut into ½-inch pieces
1 large or 2 small celery root, peeled and diced
2 carrots, peeled and sliced
2 tomatoes, peeled, seeded, and diced
1 garlic clove, crushed
½ cup shelled peas
3 tablespoons flour
6 cups beef stock
1 teaspoon Italian seasoning
Salt
Coarse black pepper

In a Dutch oven or heavy pot, sauté the bratwurst in the bacon fat until they are light brown. Remove the bratwurst, slice them, and set aside. Add the onion, zucchini, celery root, carrots, tomatoes, garlic and peas to the pot. Cook, stirring frequently, for 10 minutes. Sprinkle the flour over the vegetables and cook for 2 more minutes, stirring constantly. Heat the stock and add it gradually, continuing to stir the mixture until it reaches a boil. Add the Italian seasoning. Reduce the heat, cover, and simmer for 1½ hours. Add the reserved bratwurst slices, and salt and pepper to taste.

SERVES 6 · Approximately 200 to 225 calories each serving

12

Onion Soup with Poached Egg Oporto
Fruited Gelatin with Vanilla Cream
Tea or Coffee with Approved Artificial Sweetener
and Skim Milk

Onion Soup with Poached Egg Oporto

- 2 large yellow onions, sliced thin
- 2 teaspoons butter
- 2 teaspoons oil
- 2 tablespoons flour
- 6 teaspoons beef concentrate or 6 beef bouillon cubes (or more to taste), dissolved in 6 cups water
- Salt and pepper
- 6 small slices of French bread, about ½ inch thick, toasted
- 6 tablespoons freshly grated Parmesan cheese
- 1 cup coarse-grated Gruyère cheese
- 2 tablespoons port
- 6 poached eggs

In a heavy saucepan, sauté the onions slowly in the butter and oil until they begin to turn brown. Sprinkle with flour and add the bouillon gradually, stirring constantly. Simmer very slowly for 45 minutes. Add salt and pepper to taste.

Place a slice of the toasted bread in each of 6 individual soup casseroles. Sprinkle the Parmesan cheese and half of the Gruyère over the toast. Ladle the soup over the toast and cheese, sprinkle with remaining Gruyère, and bake in a preheated 375°F. oven for 15 minutes. Add 1 teaspoon of port to each casserole, place a poached egg on each portion, and serve. (The eggs should be warm: if they are prepared ahead of time, keep them in hot water.)

SERVES 6 · Approximately 190 to 210 calories each serving

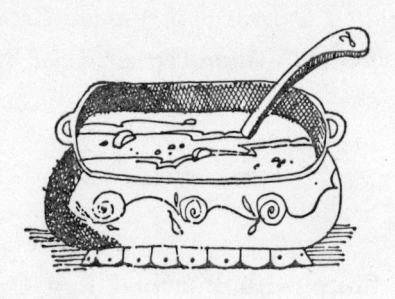

Fruited Gelatin with Vanilla Cream

- 2 packages (4 servings each) low-calorie orange-flavored gelatin dessert
- 2 cups diced pears or peaches
- 1 egg yolk
- 1 tablespoon sugar
- 1 teaspoon cornstarch
- ¾ cup skim milk
- ½ teaspoon vanilla extract

Prepare the gelatin and add the fruit according to package directions. Pour into 6 custard cups that have been rinsed in cold water and chill until firm.

In a saucepan, mix the egg yolk, sugar and cornstarch. Gradually add the milk and cook over low heat, stirring constantly, until the custard thickens. Remove from the heat, add the vanilla, and cool the sauce.

Unmold the gelatin onto 6 dessert plates. Serve the sauce separately.

SERVES 6 · Approximately 60 to 70 calories each serving

PROTEIN

1 *Escarole with Rye Croutons 79
   Roast Leg of Lamb
   *Two-Tone Squash Sauté 79
   *Creamy Cottage-Cheese Pie 80

2 Crab Fingers with Cocktail Sauce
   *Breast of Chicken Fricassee 81
   *Three Beans Cathay 82
   Steamed Carrots
   Pear with Crema Danica Cheese

3 Melon and Prosciutto
   *Veal Jerez 83
   *Green Beans and Tomatoes 84
   *Asparagus Hong Kong 84
   *Polka Dot Soufflés in Orange Shells 85

4 *Claret Consommé 86
   *Broiled Scampi 86
   *Janet Rather's Zucchini Bake 87
   Gorgonzola Cheese with Crackers

   (* indicates recipe is given)

DINNERS

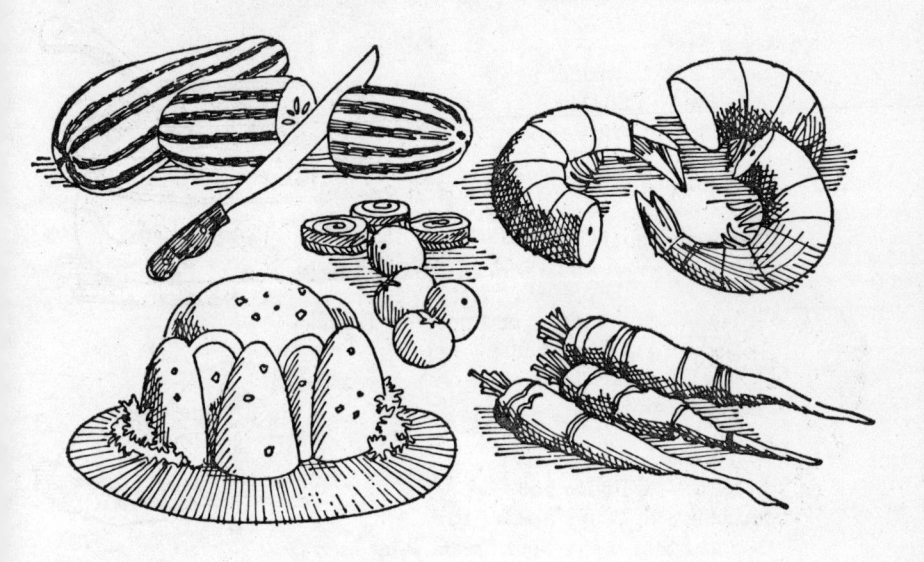

5 Oysters on the Half Shell
   * Truffled Rock Cornish Game Hens 88
   * Broccoli Amsterdam 89
   * Fresh Peaches and Black Cherries in Champagne 89

6 * Tomato-Juice Cocktail on the Rocks 90
   * Rock Cornish Game Hens Foligni 91
   * Celery and Tomatoes, Farmhouse Style 91
     Braised Escarole
   * Swedish Orange-Lemon Fromage 92

7 Westphalian Ham with Cantaloupe Balls
   * Parsleyed Veal Timbales with Parsley Sauce 93
     Steamed Leaf Spinach
   * Strawberry Blossoms 94

8 Endive and Watercress with Mustard Dressing
   * Fillet of Beef Bordelaise 95
   * Ruth Olin's Steamed Mushrooms 96
   * $2.50 Strawberries 96

(* indicates recipe is given)

9   Green Salad with Gorgonzola Dressing
    * Baked Chicken Italiano   97
    * Eggplant Provençal   98
    * Omelettes Soufflés with Raspberries   98

10 Clam Broth
    * Baked Fish Cachalot   99
    * Wax-Bean Salad   100
    * Fruits in Port Wine   101

11 * Cherry Tomato Hors-d'oeuvre   102
    * Boiled Beef in Dill Sauce   102
    Steamed Kohlrabi
    Yellow Delicious Apple with a Ripe Brie Cheese

12 Cottage-Cheese Canapés on Cucumber Rounds
    * Braised Veal in Caper Sauce   104
    * Carrots Flamande   104
    * Port and Pepper Berries   105

13 Jellied Chicken Consommé
    * Swedish Veal Rolls   106
    * Zucchini with Poppy Seeds   107
    * Pear and Strawberry Sour-Cream Ring   107

14 Spinach Salad
    * Tongue in Piquant Sauce   108
    * Magyar Kohlrabi   109
    * Salzburg Soufflés   110

15 * Cucumber Soup   111
    * Spiced Lamb Steaks Indienne   112
    * Leeks Neuchâtel   113
    * Zabaglione   113

16 * Chicken Livers in Aspic   114
    * Baked Halibut Italienne   115
    * Some-Like-It-Hot Salad   115
    Chilled Melon

17 * Mushroom and Watercress Salad   116
    * Grilled Lamb and Peppers en Brochette   117
    * Cauliflower Italian Style   118
    Pineapple Strawberry Mold

18 * Consommé with Egg Slices   119
    * Rolled Fillet of Flounder in Tomato Cups   119
    * Shortcut Horseradish Ring   120
    Red Delicious Apple with a Small Portion of Dessert Cheese

1

* Escarole with Rye Croutons
Roast Leg of Lamb
* Two-Tone Squash Sauté
* Creamy Cottage-Cheese Pie
Tea or Coffee with Approved Artificial Sweetener
and Skim Milk

Escarole with Rye Croutons

1 head of escarole
2 slices of rye bread, cut into small dices
4 teaspoons oil
Low-calorie salad dressing
1½ teaspoons caraway seeds, optional

Trim the escarole and cut off any tough outer leaves. Wash and drain the escarole and crisp in the refrigerator. Sauté the croutons in the oil until crisp and golden. Just before serving time, break the escarole into bite-size pieces, place in a salad bowl, and toss with any prepared low-calorie dressing that you prefer. Scatter the croutons over the escarole, and sprinkle with caraway seeds if desired.

SERVES 6 · Approximately 45 to 55 calories each serving

Two-Tone Squash Sauté

1 pound tender young zucchini
1 pound tender young summer squash
2 teaspoons butter
1 teaspoon oil

1 garlic clove, mashed
½ teaspoon dried orégano
Salt and pepper

Trim off the ends of the zucchini and summer squash, and slice them into bite-size pieces. Heat a heavy skillet over high heat, add the butter and oil, and when it is hot add the vegetables. Cook, stirring and turning the vegetables constantly, until they are golden. Add the garlic and orégano, lower the heat a little and cook, stirring frequently, for 10 minutes, or until the vegetables are just tender. Add salt and pepper to taste.

SERVES 6 · Approximately 35 to 40 calories each serving

Creamy Cottage-Cheese Pie

½ teaspoon butter
3 tablespoons graham-cracker crumbs
⅛ teaspoon ground cinnamon
1¾ cups cream-style cottage cheese
4 teaspoons cornstarch
⅓ cup sugar
1 teaspoon vanilla extract
Grated rind of ½ lemon
1 teaspoon lemon juice
2 eggs, separated
¼ cup sour cream

Spread the butter over the bottom and sides of a 9-inch pie plate and sprinkle with the graham-cracker crumbs mixed with the cinnamon. Place the remaining ingredients except the egg whites and the sour cream in an electric mixer and beat until smooth. Beat the egg whites until stiff but not dry, and fold into the cheese mixture. Pour into the pie plate and bake in a preheated 350°F. oven for 25 minutes. Cool, but do not chill. Drop small dabs of sour cream, evenly spaced, around the edge of the cooled pie.

SERVES 6 · Approximately 160 to 175 calories each serving

2

Crab Fingers with Cocktail Sauce
* Breast of Chicken Fricassee
* Three Beans Cathay
Steamed Carrots
Pear with a Wedge of Crema Danica
or other Dessert Cheese
Tea or Coffee with Approved Artificial Sweetener
and Skim Milk

Breast of Chicken Fricassee

1½ cups chicken stock, or 2 chicken bouillon cubes dissolved in 1½ cups water
1 leek, including a little of the green part, washed and sliced
2 celery ribs, sliced
2 carrots, scraped and sliced
3 whole breasts (6 halves) of 3- to 3½-pound fryers, without wings
1½ tablespoons flour
2 tablespoons evaporated milk, undiluted
Juice of ½ lemon
Salt and white pepper
1 tablespoon chopped parsley

Bring the stock to a boil. Add the leek, celery and carrots, cover, and cook over low heat until the vegetables are crisply tender. Add the chicken and poach, covered, over low heat for about 20 minutes, or until tender. Pour off the stock and reserve. Transfer the chicken and vegetables to a platter. Mix the flour and evaporated milk in a small saucepan. Add the lemon juice and reserved chicken stock, and cook over low heat until thickened. Season with salt and pepper to taste. Pour over the chicken and vegetables, sprinkle with parsley, and serve immediately.

SERVES 6 · Approximately 300 to 350 calories each serving

Three Beans Cathay

- 1 package (9 ounces) frozen green beans
- 1 package (9 ounces) frozen wax beans
- 3 scallions, including a little of the green part, cut into thin slices
- 2 teaspoons oil
- 1 tablespoon soy sauce
- 1-pound can of bean sprouts, well drained

Cook the frozen green beans and wax beans according to package directions, drain, and set aside. Sauté the scallions in the oil over low heat until they are tender. Stir in the soy sauce, and add the drained cooked beans and the drained bean sprouts. Heat all together, stirring constantly, until all the vegetables are hot and well mixed.

SERVES 6 · Approximately 60 to 70 calories each serving

3

Melon and Prosciutto
*Veal Jerez
* Green Beans and Tomatoes
* Asparagus Hong Kong
* Polka Dot Soufflés in Orange Shells
Tea or Coffee with Approved Artificial Sweetener and Skim Milk

Veal Jerez

- 12 thin slices of leg of veal, about 4 by 3 inches and ¼ inch thick
- 1 tablespoon butter
- 1 tablespoon oil
- ¼ cup dry sherry
- 1 garlic clove, mashed
- ½ cup minced fresh mushrooms
- 1 tablespoon Escoffier Sauce Robert
- 2 tablespoons flour
- 2 cups chicken stock, or 2 chicken bouillon cubes dissolved in 2 cups water
- 1 bay leaf
- Salt and pepper

Pound the veal between pieces of butcher's paper until it is very thin, or have the butcher pound the meat for you. Heat a heavy skillet, melt the butter with the oil, and brown the meat on both sides. Do not crowd the pan lest the meat steam. Rather brown the meat in 2 batches. Pour the sherry over the veal; remove the meat and set aside. Add the garlic and mushrooms to the skillet, and cook for 1 minute. Blend in the Escoffier Sauce and the flour. Gradually add the chicken stock, stirring constantly until it boils. Add the bay leaf and the veal, cover, and simmer for 15 to 20 minutes, or until the meat is tender. Discard the bay leaf. Add salt and pepper to taste.

SERVES 6 · Approximately 300 to 350 calories each serving

Green Beans and Tomatoes

½ cup minced onion
½ tablespoon butter
1 cup canned Italian plum tomatoes, crushed
1 pound green beans, trimmed and cut into ¾-inch lengths
1 tablespoon water
1 small garlic clove, mashed
½ teaspoon salt
½ teaspoon sugar
Dash of white pepper

Sauté the onion in the butter in a heavy saucepan over low heat until the onion is translucent. Add the remaining ingredients and simmer, tightly covered, for 30 minutes, or until the beans are tender. Adjust seasonings.

SERVES 6 · Approximately 45 to 50 calories each serving

Asparagus Hong Kong

2 pounds fresh asparagus, trimmed, or 3 packages (10 ounces each) frozen asparagus spears
2 tablespoons peanut oil or other vegetable oil
2 teaspoons soy sauce
2 teaspoons lemon juice
1 teaspoon monosodium glutamate (MSG)

Peel the trimmed fresh asparagus with a vegetable peeler, and cut into ¼-inch-thick diagonal slices. (Or, slice the frozen asparagus with a very sharp knife into ¼-inch-thick diagonal slices.) Heat a heavy skillet, add the oil, and sauté the asparagus, stirring constantly, until the pieces start to brown. Cover and cook for 2 or 3 minutes, or until the asparagus is crisply tender. Stir in the soy sauce, lemon juice and MSG, and serve the asparagus immediately.

SERVES 6 · Approximately 50 to 60 calories each serving

Polka Dot Soufflés in Orange Shells

>   6 medium-size oranges, or 3 very large oranges cut into halves
>   3 tablespoons sugar
>   2 tablespoons flour
>   ⅓ cup milk
>   2 teaspoons Cointreau or Triple Sec
>   3 eggs, separated
>   6 maraschino cherries, drained and minced
>   2 tablespoons orange marmalade

Cut off the tops of the oranges and scoop out the pulp. With a spoon, scrape out as much pith as possible to leave a clean shell. Be careful not to pierce the skin. Drain the orange pulp, reserving 2 tablespoons juice. Chop and reserve 6 tablespoons pulp.

Combine the sugar, flour, milk, and 2 tablespoons reserved orange juice in a small saucepan. Cook over low heat, stirring constantly, until the sauce becomes thick. Remove from the heat and stir in the Cointreau, egg yolks and cherries. Beat the egg whites until stiff but not dry, and fold into the cherry mixture. Put a portion of the orange pulp and marmalade in the bottom of each orange shell. Spoon the soufflé mixture on top. Place the filled shells on a baking sheet and bake in a preheated 375°F. oven for 17 minutes, or until puffed and lightly tinged with brown. Arrange on individual dishes and serve at once. (If some of the soufflé has risen over the top of an orange and spilled to one side, scoop it up with a spatula as you transfer the shells to a plate.) These soufflés may also be baked in custard cups instead of orange shells.

SERVES 6 · Approximately 145 to 165 calories each serving

4

Claret Consommé
Broiled Scampi
Janet Rather's Zucchini Bake
Gorgonzola Cheese with Crackers
(*both in discreet amounts*)
Tea or Coffee with Approved Artificial Sweetener
and Skim Milk

Claret Consommé

1 can (10½ ounces) concentrated beef consommé
6 thin orange slices
6 tablespoons claret

Dilute the consommé with water as directed on the can and bring to the boiling point. Place 1 slice of orange and 1 tablespoon claret in each of 6 heated bouillon cups. Add the hot consommé and serve immediately.

SERVES 6 · Approximately 25 to 30 calories each serving

Broiled Scampi

36 very large shrimps (about 8 to 10 to the pound)
2 tablespoons butter
1 teaspoon garlic powder
1 teaspoon salt
½ teaspoon coarse black pepper
2 teaspoons prepared mustard

1½ tablespoons lemon juice
¼ cup dry white wine
1 tablespoon minced parsley

Peel the shrimps, leaving the tail shell. Split the shrimps almost through, along the intestinal vein. Remove any bits of dirt or vein. Melt the butter in a tiny saucepan and stir in the remaining ingredients except for the parsley. Line the broiler pan with foil and oil the foil lightly. Place the shrimps on the foil in a single layer and brush them with the butter mixture. Broil in the preheated broiler for 5 to 8 minutes, or until shrimps are opaque and beginning to fleck with brown. Transfer to a serving platter and spoon any leftover sauce over the shrimps. Sprinkle with parsley and serve immediately.

SERVES 6 · Approximately 300 to 315 calories each serving

Janet Rather's Zucchini Bake

2 slices of lean bacon, cut into 1-inch squares
3 medium-size onions, peeled and cut into thin slices
2 pounds young zucchini, cut into ⅓-inch-thick slices
Salt
Coarse black pepper
1 teaspoon dried basil
¼ cup catsup

Sauté the bacon until partially brown but not crisp. Remove the bacon pieces and set aside. Add the onions to the skillet and sauté, stirring constantly, until they start to color. Place a layer of zucchini in a baking dish and spoon in a portion of the onion. Sprinkle lightly with salt, pepper and basil, and dot with catsup. (It is impossible to give exact amounts of salt or pepper, for this varies according to the saltiness of the bacon fat and the strength of the pepper.) Repeat these layers. Place the reserved bacon on top and bake, covered, in a preheated 350°F. oven for 45 minutes.

SERVES 6 · Approximately 95 to 110 calories each serving

5

Oysters on the Half Shell
* Truffled Rock Cornish Game Hens
* Broccoli Amsterdam
* Fresh Peaches and Black Cherries in Champagne
Tea or Coffee with Approved Artificial Sweetener
and Skim Milk

Truffled Rock Cornish Game Hens

1 tablespoon minced truffle or truffle peelings
2 tablespoons Madeira
3 large Rock Cornish Game hens, split into halves, or 6 small whole birds
Salt and pepper
2 tablespoons butter
2 teaspoons oil
2 chicken bouillon cubes dissolved in 1 cup water
1 tablespoon heavy cream

Marinate the truffle in the Madeira for 30 minutes. Sprinkle the hens with salt and pepper. Set aside the hen livers. Brown the hens in half of the butter mixed with the oil in a large heavy skillet. Remove the hens and deglaze the skillet with the chicken bouillon. Replace the hens, cover, and simmer for 35 to 45 minutes, or until they are tender. Or roast in a preheated 400°F. oven for about the same length of time.

Sauté the reserved livers in the remaining butter until they are lightly browned but still pink inside. Chop them into coarse pieces and add them to the juices in the pan in which the hens were cooked. Add the cream, and purée the mixture in a blender or force it through a fine sieve. Add the truffles and their marinade and heat, but do not boil. Arrange the hens on a serving platter. Serve the sauce separately.

SERVES 6 · Approximately 275 to 300 calories each serving

Broccoli Amsterdam

1 bunch of broccoli (about 2 pounds)
½ tablespoon melted chicken, duck, or goose fat
2 tablespoons flour
½ teaspoon nutmeg, freshly grated if possible
Salt and pepper

Cut off the flowerets of the broccoli; peel the stems and dice them. Cook the diced stems in boiling salted water for a few minutes, or until just tender. Add the flowerets and cook for a few minutes longer. Drain the broccoli and reserve the liquid. Chop the cooked vegetable fine. In a saucepan heat the fat, blend in the flour, and cook for 1 minute. Gradually add ¼ cup of the reserved liquid and cook, stirring constantly, until the sauce is very thick. Add the nutmeg, and salt and pepper to taste. Fold in the broccoli, adding more liquid if necessary. Adjust seasonings.

SERVES 6 · Approximately 45 to 55 calories each serving

Fresh Peaches and Black Cherries in Champagne

6 peaches
3 tablespoons sugar
⅓ cup water
12 black cherries
¾ cup champagne

Scald the peaches and slip off the skins. Heat the sugar and water to the boiling point. Lower the heat and poach the peaches gently for 4 to 5 minutes. (Although this seems a small amount of liquid for poaching, the fruit will quickly release enough juices to make adequate fruit syrup.) Cool and chill. Shortly before serving time, place 1 peach and 2 cherries in a champagne glass. Add the champagne to the fruit syrup and pour over the fruit.

SERVES 6 · Approximately 80 to 95 calories each serving

6

Tomato-Juice Cocktail on the Rocks
Rock Cornish Game Hens Foligni
Celery and Tomatoes, Farmhouse Style
Braised Escarole (Use just a touch of oil
in a nonstick skillet.)
Swedish Orange-Lemon Fromage
Tea or Coffee with Approved Artificial Sweetener
and Skim Milk

Tomato-Juice Cocktail on the Rocks

3 cups tomato-juice cocktail
1 tablespoon catsup
1 tablespoon Escoffier Sauce Robert
Salt and white pepper
1 scallion, white part only, cut into thin slices

Place all ingredients except the scallion in a cocktail shaker filled with ice. Place 2 ice cubes in each of 6 old-fashioned glasses. Shake the cocktail shaker vigorously to mix the ingredients thoroughly. Pour into the glasses and sprinkle a few slices of scallion on top of each cocktail.

SERVES 6 · Approximately 35 to 40 calories each serving

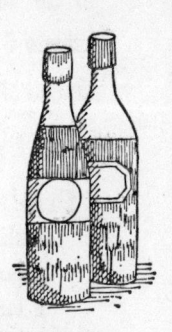

Rock Cornish Game Hens Foligni

3 large Rock Cornish Game hens, cut into halves
Salt
6 small white onions, each stuck with 2 cloves
1 lemon, sliced
2 ounces prosciutto, cut into strips
2 teaspoons tomato paste
1 tablespoon vinegar
2 tablespoons olive oil
¼ teaspoon coarse black pepper
¾ teaspoon ground cinnamon

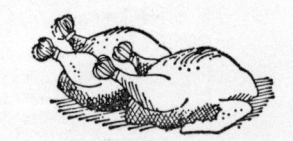

Sprinkle the hens with salt, and place them in a single layer in a roasting pan with a cover. Arrange the onions, lemon slices and ham over the hens. Mix the tomato paste, vinegar, oil, pepper and cinnamon, and spoon over the hens. Cover tightly; if the pan cover is not tight-fitting, cover with a piece of foil. Roast in a preheated 350°F. oven for 45 to 55 minutes, or until the hens are tender. Place the hens on a serving platter. Discard the cloves and lemon slices. Spoon the remaining garniture over the hens and pour any pan juices over all.

SERVES 6 · Approximately 265 to 290 calories each serving

Celery and Tomatoes, Farmhouse Style

1 slice of lean bacon, minced
1 large onion, minced
1 large bunch of celery
1 pound tomatoes, peeled, seeded, and chopped
Salt and pepper
2 teaspoons flour
2 tablespoons cold water

In a heavy saucepan, sauté the bacon until crisp. Remove the bacon pieces and reserve. In the drippings, sauté the onion until tender and golden. Trim and scrape the celery, discard the leaves, and cut the celery into ½-inch pieces. Add the celery to the onion and cook over high heat for 2 minutes, stirring constantly. Add the tomatoes, reduce the heat and simmer, covered, for 1½ to 2 hours. Add salt and pepper to taste. Mix the flour and water until there are no lumps, blend into the pan juices, and cook until they thicken a little. Pour into a serving bowl and sprinkle with the reserved bacon.

SERVES 6 · Approximately 45 to 55 calories each serving

Swedish Orange-Lemon Fromage

- 2 teaspoons unflavored gelatin
- 2 tablespoons water
- 2 tablespoons orange juice
- 1 tablespoon lemon juice
- 1 teaspoon grated orange rind
- 4 eggs, separated
- 7 tablespoons sugar

Soak the gelatin in the water in a small pot for 5 minutes. Dissolve over low heat, then set aside to cool. Stir in the orange juice, lemon juice, and grated rind. Beat the egg yolks and sugar until thick and light. Beat in the gelatin mixture. Beat the egg whites until stiff but not dry and fold into the yolk mixture. Spoon into 6 individual dessert saucers and chill until serving time.

SERVES 6 · Approximately 110 to 120 calories each serving

7

Westphalian Ham with Cantaloupe Balls
* Parsleyed Veal Timbales with Parsley Sauce
Steamed Leaf Spinach
* Strawberry Blossoms
*Tea or Coffee with Approved Artificial Sweetener
and Skim Milk*

Parsleyed Veal Timbales with Parsley Sauce

1 medium-size onion, minced
1 teaspoon butter
2 eggs, lightly beaten
1 teaspoon salt
Dash of white pepper
2 tablespoons minced parsley
2 tablespoons evaporated milk, undiluted
¼ cup fine dry bread crumbs
¼ cup water
2 pounds leg of veal, ground

Sauté the onion in the butter until golden. Put the eggs, salt, pepper, parsley, evaporated milk, bread crumbs and water in a bowl. Add the sautéed onion and the ground veal, and mix until well blended. Divide the mixture among 6 buttered timbale molds or custard cups, and place the molds in a shallow baking pan containing ½ inch of water. Cover the pan with foil and bake the timbales in a preheated 400°F. oven for 45 minutes. Unmold the timbales onto a serving platter or individual plates. Spoon a bit of the sauce over each timbale and serve the remainder in a sauceboat.

Parsley Sauce

1 tablespoon butter
2 tablespoons flour
2½ cups chicken stock
2 tablespoons Parmesan cheese
2 tablespoons evaporated milk mixed with 1 teaspoon flour
Salt and pepper
¼ cup minced parsley

Melt the butter in a saucepan, stir in the flour, and gradually add the stock, stirring constantly. Bring the sauce to a boil and cook it until it is reduced by one quarter. Add the Parmesan cheese and the evaporated milk and flour. Bring to a boil and cook, stirring constantly, until the sauce thickens. Remove from the heat, adjust the seasonings to taste, and stir in the minced parsley.

SERVES 6 · Approximately 425 to 475 calories each serving

Strawberry Blossoms

36 very large ripe strawberries, hulled
½ cup creamed cottage cheese
Sugar, optional

Starting from the tip, cut the strawberries almost into halves, to, but not through the stem ends. Cut again, at a right angle to the first cut. Gently press the berry so as to open up the 4 "petals."

Mash the cottage cheese and add sugar if desired. Spoon a small amount of the cheese in the center of each "blossom." Arrange 6 blossoms on each dessert plate. Chill until serving time.

SERVES 6 · Approximately 35 to 50 calories each serving

8

Endive and Watercress with Mustard Dressing
* Fillet of Beef Bordelaise
* Ruth Olin's Steamed Mushrooms
* Two-Dollar-and-Fifty-Cent Strawberries
*Tea or Coffee with Approved Artificial Sweetener
and Skim Milk*

Fillet of Beef Bordelaise

1 small onion, minced
1 tablespoon butter
2½ tablespoons flour
2 cups beef consommé
¼ cup red Bordeaux wine
1 garlic clove, mashed
¼ cup catsup
2 teaspoons Worcestershire sauce
½ teaspoon celery salt
1½ teaspoons sugar
½ teaspoon salt
2½ pounds beef fillet (tenderloin)
1 tablespoon oil
1 tablespoon minced parsley

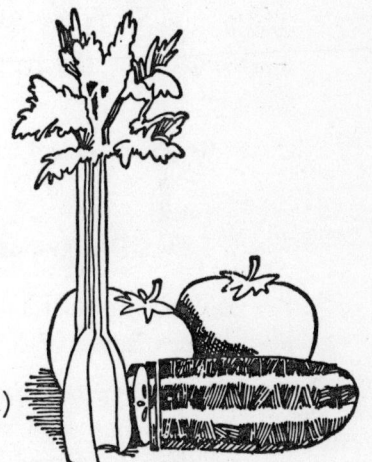

In a heavy saucepan, over medium heat, sauté the onion in the butter until it is translucent. Add the flour and cook, stirring constantly, until light brown. Gradually add the beef consommé and the wine, and stir over medium heat until the sauce is smooth. Add the garlic, catsup, Worcestershire sauce, celery salt, sugar and salt. Simmer, covered, for 30 minutes, stirring frequently.

Trim the fat from the beef and cut the meat into diagonal slices ¼ inch thick. Heat a large heavy skillet over high heat. Add the oil and sear the slices on both sides. Remove the slices from the pan. Stir the sauce into the pan with any accumulated juices from the meat. Cook for 2 minutes, then replace the meat in the pan, making sure to coat each slice on both sides with the sauce. Cook for 1 minute, or until the meat is thoroughly heated but not overcooked. Sprinkle with parsley and serve immediately.

SERVES 6 · Approximately 400 to 425 calories each serving

Ruth Olin's Steamed Mushrooms

1 pound firm white mushrooms
1 tablespoon butter
½ teaspoon salt

Cut off the stems flush with the mushroom caps. Cut the stems and the caps into thin slices. Melt the butter in the top of a double boiler; add the salt and the sliced mushrooms. Toss the mushrooms with the butter, cover the pan, and steam for 20 minutes.

SERVES 6 · Approximately 35 to 40 calories each serving

Two-Dollar-and-Fifty-Cent Strawberries

For that is the price at a very posh restaurant for their version of Strawberries Romanoff.

3 cups fully ripe strawberries
2 tablespoons sugar
2 tablespoons Grand Marnier
2 cups vanilla ice milk
⅓ cup Cool Whip or other low-calorie whipped topping

Partially crush the strawberries with a fork, add the sugar and Grand Marnier, and chill for 1 hour or longer. Shortly before serving time, soften the ice milk and fold into the berries. Fold in the whipped topping. Spoon into a serving bowl or 6 individual dessert dishes and serve immediately.

SERVES 6 · Approximately 125 to 145 calories each serving

9

Green Salad with Gorgonzola Dressing
*(Add a little crumbled Gorgonzola cheese
to a low-calorie salad dressing.)*
* *Baked Chicken Italiano*
* *Eggplant Provençal*
* *Omelettes Soufflés with Raspberries*
*Tea or Coffee with Approved Artificial Sweetener
and Skim Milk*

Baked Chicken Italiano

6 chicken quarters, from 3- to 3½-pound fryers, dark or light meat
1 large lemon, or 1½ medium-size lemons, quartered
1½ teaspoons Lawry's Seasoned Salt
6 tablespoons low-calorie Italian dressing, or any preferred low-calorie dressing

Cut off the wing tips (if you are using white meat), and remove any fat from the inside of the chicken pieces. Squeeze the lemon directly onto the chicken and rub the juice in with the lemon pieces. Place the chicken in a single layer in a shallow baking dish. Sprinkle with the seasoned salt. Pour the dressing over all. Bake in a preheated 375°F. oven for 45 minutes, basting frequently. Raise the heat to 475°F. and bake for an additional 15 minutes, basting twice.

SERVES 6 · Approximately 200 to 240 calories each serving

Eggplant Provencal

1 eggplant, about 1½ pounds
Salt
1 large onion, chopped
1 large green pepper, seeded and cut into strips
1 tablespoon bacon fat
2 medium-size tomatoes, peeled and chopped
1 garlic clove, crushed
1 teaspoon dried orégano
1 teaspoon dried basil
⅛ teaspoon coarse black pepper
1 large canned pimiento, drained and cut into thin strips
2 tablespoons drained capers

Peel the eggplant, cut into ½-inch cubes, sprinkle generously with salt, and let stand for 30 minutes. Sauté the onion and pepper in the bacon fat over medium heat for 15 minutes, stirring constantly. Dry the eggplant in paper towels and add to the onion mixture with the tomatoes, garlic, orégano, basil and pepper. Cook covered, stirring frequently, for about 20 minutes, or until the eggplant is tender. Drain off any excess juice. Add salt to taste and spoon into a shallow baking dish that can come to the table. Garnish the top of the vegetables with pimiento strips and capers, and place in a preheated 425°F. oven until bubbling. Serve piping hot, or chill and serve cold.

SERVES 6 · Approximately 95 to 115 calories each serving

Omelettes Soufflés with Raspberries

9 egg whites
9 tablespoons sugar
6 egg yolks
1½ cups fresh ripe raspberries
⅓ cup low-calorie raspberry or strawberry jam

In the large bowl of an electric mixer, beat the egg whites until foamy. Gradually add 6 tablespoons of the sugar and continue beating until the meringue is thick and glossy. In a small bowl beat the egg yolks with the remaining sugar until the mixture is thick and light. Fold the yolk mixture into the meringue. Spoon the mixture into 6 buttered large shirred-egg dishes, or onto 2 buttered baking sheets, dividing the mixture into 6 equal mounds. With a spatula, shape them into high, smooth ovals. Bake the omelettes in a preheated 300°F. oven for 10 minutes. Remove them from the oven. If you have baked the omelettes on baking sheets, carefully transfer them to individual plates. Wet a small sharp knife, and make a lengthwise incision in the top of each omelette, about 4 inches long and 1 inch deep. Mix the raspberries with the jam and fill into the omelettes. Serve at once. (These omelettes may also be baked in individual soup casseroles.)

SERVES 6 · Approximately 170 to 180 calories each serving

10

Clam Broth
* Baked Fish Cachalot
* Wax-Bean Salad
* Fruits in Port Wine
Tea or Coffee with Approved Artificial Sweetener
and Skim Milk

Baked Fish Cachalot

2 pounds sole or flounder fillets
Salt
⅔ cup dry white wine

2 cans (4 ounces each) mushroom stems and pieces
½ cup skim milk
1 tablespoon butter
¼ cup flour
8 drops of Tabasco
1 teaspoon Worcestershire sauce
2 tablespoons catsup
¼ cup grated Parmesan cheese
1 large tomato, peeled, seeded, and cut into julienne strips
2 tablespoons light cream
2 tablespoons minced parsley

Fold each piece of fish in half and arrange the pieces in a single layer in a shallow oven-to-table baking dish. Sprinkle with ½ teaspoon salt and pour the wine over the fish. Bake uncovered in a preheated 375°F. oven for 12 minutes, or until the fish flakes easily with a fork. Drain the stock and reserve. Drain the mushroom juice and add to the fish stock with the skim milk. Measure the liquid and add water, if necessary, to make 2¼ cups liquid in all.

In a saucepan sauté the mushrooms in the butter for 2 minutes. Sprinkle with flour and add the liquid gradually, stirring constantly until the sauce thickens. Add the Tabasco, Worcestershire, catsup and cheese. Season with salt to taste. Scatter the tomato strips over the fish. Remove the sauce from the heat, stir in the light cream, and pour over the fish. Cool and refrigerate until shortly before serving time. Bake in a preheated 375°F. oven for 25 minutes, or until bubbling. Sprinkle with parsley.

SERVES 6 · Approximately 345 to 365 calories each serving

Wax-Bean Salad

3 tablespoons sour cream
1 tablespoon Escoffier Sauce Diable
1 tablespoon cider vinegar
1½ tablespoons catsup
¼ teaspoon salt

Grinding of coarse black pepper
4 cups cold cooked wax beans, cut into ¾-inch pieces
1 tablespoon minced parsley

Mix the sour cream, Escoffier Sauce, vinegar, catsup, salt and pepper. Toss this dressing with the wax beans and marinate for 1 hour. Stir occasionally. Add the parsley and refrigerate until serving time.

SERVES 6 · Approximately 40 to 50 calories each serving

Fruits in Port Wine

2 pounds fully ripe peaches
2 tablespoons sugar
2 tablespoons white port
1 medium-size cantaloupe
1 cup blueberries

Scald the peaches and slip off the skins. Mix the sugar and wine in a saucepan and heat slowly, stirring constantly, until the sugar dissolves. Remove from the heat and slice the peaches into the saucepan. (The peaches will release juices to make enough syrup.) Raise the heat and cook the peaches, covered, for about 5 minutes, or until the fruit is just tender. Scoop out as many melon balls as possible and add to the hot peaches. Stir in the blueberries, cool, and chill.

SERVES 6 · Approximately 125 to 135 calories each serving

11

Cherry Tomato Hors-d'oeuvre
Boiled Beef in Dill Sauce
Steamed Kohlrabi
Yellow Delicious Apple with a Ripe Brie Cheese
Tea or Coffee with Approved Artificial Sweetener
and Skim Milk

~~~~

Cherry Tomato Hors-d'oeuvre

For each hors-d'oeuvre:
1 cherry tomato
1 rolled anchovy
¼ teaspoon seasoned bread crumbs

Cut off the tops of the tomatoes and reserve. With a small spoon scoop out the pulp, and set the tomatoes upside down to drain. Turn right side up and put 1 rolled anchovy in the bottom of each tomato. Moisten the bread crumbs with a little of the anchovy oil and put about ¼ teaspoon of the mixture into each tomato. Replace the tops of the tomatoes, and bake them on a baking sheet in a preheated 400°F. oven for 5 minutes. Serve immediately.

Approximately 20 calories for each hors-d'oeuvre

Boiled Beef in Dill Sauce

2½ to 2¾ pounds beef bottom round
1 veal knuckle, cracked
2 large carrots, scraped and cut into 1-inch pieces

3 celery ribs, with a few of the leaves, cut into ½-inch slices
6 small white onions, peeled
1 yellow onion, peeled and chopped
1 parsley root, trimmed and cut into pieces
Salt
White pepper
2 teaspoons butter
2 tablespoons flour
3 tablespoons minced fresh dill

Place the beef, veal knuckle, carrots, celery, white onions, yellow onion and parsley root in a soup kettle. Pour in 2½ quarts water, 1 teaspoon salt, and ⅛ teaspoon white pepper; bring to a boil. Skim off the scum, reduce the heat and simmer, covered, for 2½ hours, or until tender. Discard the veal knuckle. Keep the meat warm while making the sauce.

In a saucepan, melt the butter and blend in the flour. Gradually add 1½ cups of the stock and cook slowly, stirring constantly, until the sauce thickens. Add the dill and adjust seasonings. Slice the meat into a large skillet or shallow heatproof dish that can go to the table. Scatter the vegetables over the meat slices. Pour the sauce over the meat and serve immediately.

SERVES 6 · Approximately 375 to 400 calories each serving

12

Cottage-Cheese Canapés on Cucumber Rounds
(Sprinkle seasoned salt on the cheese.)
* Braised Veal in Caper Sauce
* Carrots Flamande
* Port and Pepper Berries
Tea or Coffee with Approved Artificial Sweetener
and Skim Milk

Braised Veal in Caper Sauce

3 to 3½ pounds boneless rump of veal
1 tablespoon bacon drippings
2 cups water
¼ cup dry vermouth
3 tablespoons drained capers
¼ cup light cream mixed with 2 tablespoons flour
Salt and pepper

Brown the veal in the bacon drippings over high heat. Add the water, cover, and simmer over reduced heat for several hours, or until the meat is tender. Remove the meat from the liquid and keep warm. Add the vermouth to the stock. Mash the capers with a fork and add them. Stir in a few spoonfuls of the hot stock into the cream-flour mixture, and pour back into the stock. Cook over medium heat,stirring constantly, until the sauce is thickened. Add salt and pepper to taste. Slice the meat, arrange on a serving platter, dribble a spoonful or so of sauce over the meat, and serve the remainder in a sauceboat.

Note: There is more than enough veal to serve 6 diet portions, but if you cook too small a piece, it is difficult to carve. Therefore, cook the whole piece and use the leftover veal, cold, for 2 small servings for lunch with green salad.

SERVES 6 dinners and about 2 lunches · Approximately 475 to 525 calories each serving

Carrots Flamande

6 medium-large carrots, scraped and sliced
½ tablespoon butter
1 tablespoon sugar
2 beef bouillon cubes dissolved in 1½ cups water
Salt
2 teaspoons minced parsley

Blanch the carrots in boiling salted water for 5 minutes. Drain and put them back in the saucepan in which they were blanched. Add the butter and sugar and sauté, shaking the pot very frequently, for a few minutes, until the carrots are lightly flecked with brown. Add the beef bouillon and cook, cover ajar, for 5 minutes, or until the carrots are tender and the liquid almost completely evaporated. Add salt to taste, sprinkle with parsley, and serve at once.

SERVES 6 · Approximately 45 to 55 calories each serving

Port and Pepper Berries

1 quart fully ripe strawberries
⅓ cup sugar
1½ teaspoons coarse black pepper
½ cup white port

Place the berries in a serving bowl. Sprinkle the sugar and pepper over the berries, spoon the port over all, and toss gently. Marinate for several hours, mixing occasionally.

SERVES 6 · Approximately 105 to 115 calories each serving

13

Jellied Chicken Consommé (Stir in a little minced parsley when the consommé is almost set.)
* *Swedish Veal Rolls*
* *Zucchini with Poppy Seeds*
* *Pear and Strawberry Sour-Cream Ring*
Tea or Coffee with Approved Artificial Sweetener and Skim Milk

Swedish Veal Rolls

- 3 tablespoons butter
- 2 large onions, diced fine
- 1 large carrot, diced
- 2 celery ribs, sliced fine
- 2 teaspoons salt
- ¼ teaspoon white pepper
- 1 cup chicken stock, or 1 chicken bouillon cube dissolved in 1 cup water
- 1 cup canned Italian plum tomatoes, crushed
- 1 egg, lightly beaten
- ½ pound ground beef
- 1 tablespoon minced parsley
- 12 scalloppine of veal, about 2 pounds

Melt 1 tablespoon of the butter in a heavy skillet. Add the onions, carrot and celery, and sauté over medium heat until light brown. Stir constantly. Add half of the salt, half of the pepper, the chicken stock and canned tomatoes, and bring to a boil. Reduce the heat, cover the pan, and simmer for 30 minutes, or until sauce is very thick.

In a bowl, mix the egg, beef, parsley, and remaining salt and pepper. Work the mixture with your hands until well blended.

Put a portion of the filling on one end of each veal scallop, roll them up, and secure with food picks. In a large heavy skillet, melt the remaining butter and brown the rolls on all sides. Pour the sauce over the rolls, cover, and cook slowly for 20 minutes, or until the meat is tender. Discard the food picks and serve. These rolls may be made in advance and reheated.

SERVES 6 · Approximately 475 to 500 calories each serving

Zucchini with Poppy Seeds

½ cup chopped onion
1 tablespoon vegetable oil (not olive oil)
½ teaspoon salt
½ teaspoon paprika
1 teaspoon poppy seeds
Freshly ground coarse black pepper
1½ pounds tender young zucchini
3 tablespoons sour cream

Sauté the onion in the oil in a covered heavy saucepan over low heat for 20 minutes. Do not allow the onion to brown. Add the salt, paprika, almost all the poppy seeds, and pepper to taste. Trim off the ends of the zucchini and cut them into ½-inch-thick slices. Simmer, covered, over low heat for 15 to 20 minutes, or until tender, stirring occasionally. If the vegetable has drawn much water, uncover and cook rapidly for a few minutes to evaporate the excess liquid. Transfer the zucchini to a serving bowl, spoon the sour cream on top, and sprinkle with the remaining poppy seeds.

SERVES 6 · Approximately 55 to 65 calories each serving

Pear and Strawberry Sour-Cream Ring

2 packages (4 servings each) low-calorie strawberry-flavored gelatin dessert
2 cups hot water

1 cup cold water
¾ cup sour cream
2 pears, peeled, cored, and diced
1 pint strawberries with hulls left on

Dissolve the gelatin in the hot water. Stir in the cold water and the sour cream until the mixture is well blended, or blend it in an electric blender. Chill until the mixture starts to thicken. Fold in the pears, and pour into a 5- to 6-cup ring mold that has been rinsed in cold water. Chill until set. Turn out onto a serving platter, fill the center of the ring with strawberries, and refrigerate until serving time.

SERVES 6 · Approximately 100 to 115 calories each serving

14

Spinach Salad
* Tongue in Piquant Sauce
* Magyar Kohlrabi
* Salzburg Soufflés
*Tea or Coffee with Approved Artificial Sweetener
and Skim Milk*

Tongue in Piquant Sauce

1 smoked or pickled beef tongue, about 4 pounds
6 peppercorns
1 bay leaf
2 medium-size onions, chopped fine
2 medium-size carrots, peeled and diced fine
1 tablespoon butter
2 tablespoons flour
2 cups beef stock, or 2 beef bouillon cubes dissolved in 2 cups water

2 tablespoons minced gherkins
1 tablespoon vinegar
1 tablespoon drained capers
1 teaspoon sugar

Put the tongue in a large pot, cover it with cold water, and bring to a boil. If the water becomes salty, pour it off and add fresh water. Add the peppercorns and the bay leaf and bring to a boil again. Reduce the heat and simmer, covered, for about 3 hours, or until tender. (Or cook in a pressure cooker for about 1¼ hours.)

While the tongue is cooking make the sauce: In a saucepan, sauté the onions and carrots in the butter until the onions are translucent. Remove from the heat, sprinkle the flour over the vegetables, and pour in a little of the beef stock. Stir until blended and add the remaining stock. Cook over medium heat until the sauce starts to thicken. Add the gherkins, vinegar, capers and sugar, and cook, stirring constantly, until the sauce thickens to desired consistency.

Allow the cooked tongue to cool a little; remove the skin, bones and fat. Cut 18 large slices about ¼ inch thick. Slice the tongue on the diagonal to get large slices. Place the slices in a large skillet or saucepan, cover with the sauce, and simmer together for 5 minutes, then serve.

SERVES 6 · Approximately 350 to 375 calories each serving

Magyar Kohlrabi

8 young kohlrabi
2 teaspoons rendered chicken or goose fat
1 teaspoon sugar
Pinch of white pepper
1 chicken bouillon cube dissolved in ½ cup water
Salt
2 tablespoons minced parsley
1 hard-cooked egg, chopped fine

Peel the kohlrabi and cut them into ½-inch cubes. Melt the fat in a heavy saucepan, add the sugar, and cook until the sugar turns golden. Add the kohlrabi and cook, stirring constantly, for 1 minute. Add the pepper and the chicken bouillon, cover, and cook for 15 minutes, or until the kohlrabi are tender. Uncover and cook over high heat, stirring frequently, until the liquid is almost evaporated. Add salt to taste and the parsley. Sprinkle the chopped egg over the vegetable and serve at once.

SERVES 6 · Approximately 50 to 60 calories each serving

Salzburg Soufflés

For each serving:
1 egg, separated
1 teaspoon sugar
½ teaspoon flour
Milk
Confectioners' sugar

Preheat oven to 450°F. at least 20 minutes before serving time. Beat the egg white until stiff but not dry. Beat the yolk with the sugar and flour until well blended. Fold into the beaten white. Pour enough milk into a small baking dish (or shirred-egg dish or soup casserole) to just cover the bottom. Spoon the egg mixture into the dish and smooth the surface with a spatula. Bake for about 4 minutes, or until the top begins to be flecked with brown. Do not overbake: the inside must be almost unbaked and creamy. Dust generously with confectioners' sugar, and serve immediately.

SERVES 1 · Approximately 110 to 120 calories each serving

Note: You may bake more than one portion in a large shallow baking dish, preferably one that can come to the table. For 6 portions, allow 1 to 1½ minutes longer baking time. Transfer the soufflés to individual dessert dishes with the aid of a pie server.

15

Cucumber Soup
Spiced Lamb Steaks Indienne
Leeks Neuchâtel
Zabaglione
Tea or Coffee with Approved Artificial Sweetener
and Skim Milk

Cucumber Soup

2 pounds young cucumbers
1 bunch of scallions
1 quart well-seasoned chicken consommé
1 teaspoon A.1. Sauce
2 tablespoons minced chives

Peel the cucumbers, cut them lengthwise into quarters, scrape out the seeds, and cut the cucumbers into cubes. Trim the roots of the scallions, and cut them into ¼-inch-thick slices, including about 1 inch of the green part. Simmer the cucumbers and scallions in the chicken consommé until the vegetables are tender. Add the A.1. Sauce and whirl in the blender. Adjust seasonings. Pour into 6 soup plates and sprinkle the chives on top.

SERVES 6 · Approximately 35 to 45 calories each serving

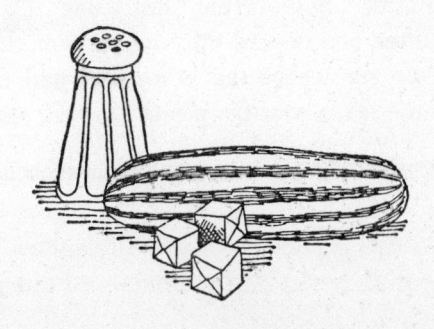

Spiced Lamb Steaks Indienne

6 thin lamb steaks
2 lamb kidneys
2 large onions, diced
2 teaspoons butter
Salt
½ teaspoon ground cuminseed
½ teaspoon ground cinnamon
½ teaspoon ground ginger
½ teaspoon ground turmeric
½ teaspoon crushed dried mint leaves
½ teaspoon sugar
Pinch of chili powder
1 garlic clove, mashed

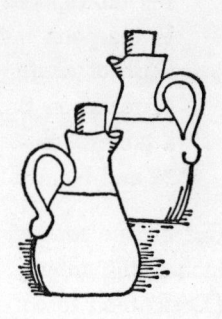

Have the butcher remove the bones from the lamb steaks and pound them thinner, if necessary, for easy folding. Remove the core from the kidneys and dice the kidneys. In a heavy skillet, sauté the onions in the butter for 3 minutes, stirring constantly, and add one quarter of the sautéed onions to the diced kidneys. Add ½ teaspoon salt. Put a spoonful of the kidney mixture on half of each lamb steak and fold over the other half. Secure with food picks or small skewers. To the remaining onions add the remaining ingredients. Cook the mixture for 5 minutes, stirring constantly. In another skillet brown the lamb steaks lightly in their own fat, or use a minimum of other fat. Add the onion mixture and 2 cups water. Bring to a boil, then reduce the heat and simmer, covered, for 1 hour, or until just tender. Place the meat on a serving platter, and discard the food picks or skewers. Skim any fat from the surface of the sauce and add more salt if needed. Spoon the sauce over the meat.

SERVES 6 · Approximately 400 to 475 calories each serving

Leeks Neuchâtel

12 medium-size leeks
1½ tablespoons butter
½ teaspoon salt
Dash of white pepper
½ teaspoon Bovril or other meat concentrate
1 tablespoon lemon juice
¾ cup Neuchâtel wine

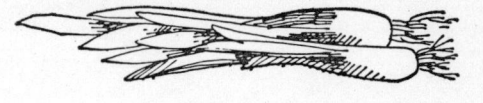

Cut off the root ends of the leeks. Trim them, leaving about 1 inch of the green part. Wash them thoroughly under cold water. (Leeks tend to collect dirt and sand which must be flushed out under running water.) Sauté the leeks in the butter in a large heavy skillet for 3 minutes, turning them almost constantly. Sprinkle the leeks with salt and pepper. Mix the meat concentrate, lemon juice and wine and pour over all. Cover and cook over low heat for 35 to 45 minutes, or until the leeks are tender. Transfer them to a serving platter. If the pan juices are lightly syrupy, pour them over the leeks. If they are watery, reduce over high heat before pouring over the vegetable.

SERVES 6 · Approximately 55 to 70 calories each serving

Zabaglione

6 egg yolks
6 tablespoons sugar
⅔ cup Marsala wine

Fill the bottom of a double boiler one-third full with hot but not boiling water, and place it over low heat. In the top of the double boiler mix the egg yolks and sugar. With a whisk or an electric beater, beat the mixture until it is thick and light. Gradually beat in the wine. Place over the hot water and beat vigorously until the mixture gets foamy and thick. Spoon into wine or champagne glasses and serve immediately.

SERVES 6 · Approximately 145 to 155 calories each serving

16

Chicken Livers in Aspic
Baked Halibut Italienne
Some-Like-It-Hot Salad
Chilled Melon
Tea or Coffee with Approved Artificial Sweetener
and Skim Milk

Chicken Livers in Aspic

1½ envelopes unflavored gelatin
2¾ cups chicken stock, or 3 chicken bouillon cubes dissolved in 2¾ cups water
2 tablespoons minced onion
2 teaspoons butter
12 chicken livers, about ¾ pound
Lettuce

Soak the gelatin in the chicken stock for 5 minutes; dissolve it over low heat. Pour a thin layer of the liquid into 6 molds or custard cups that have been rinsed in cold water and chill for a short while, until set. Meanwhile sauté the onion in the butter until translucent. Add the livers and cook, covered, over low heat for a few minutes. Turn the livers and cook them until they are pale pink inside. Remove the livers and chill in a refrigerator or freezer. Add the remaining dissolved gelatin to the pan in which the livers were cooked, strain the juices, reserve, and cool.

Place 2 livers on top of the layer of aspic in each of the

molds. Pour in the reserved juices and chill until set. Run the tip of a small knife around the edge of the aspic to loosen it. Dip the bottoms of the molds in hot water for a few seconds, turn out onto individual plates or a serving platter, and garnish with lettuce.

SERVES 6 · Approximately 110 to 125 calories each serving

Baked Halibut Italienne

- 2 large onions, sliced
- 1 tablespoon olive oil
- 3 large tomatoes, peeled and chopped
- 1/3 teaspoon ground allspice
- Salt and pepper
- 6 halibut steaks, about 6 ounces each
- 1/4 cup sliced stuffed olives

In a large skillet, sauté the onions in the oil over low heat, stirring frequently, until the onions are translucent. Add the tomatoes, raise the heat and cook, stirring constantly, until the liquid has evaporated. Add the allspice, and salt and pepper to taste. Arrange the halibut steaks side by side in a shallow baking dish that can come to the table. Sprinkle them lightly with salt and pepper and spread the tomato mixture over the top. Scatter the olives over all and bake in a preheated 375°F. oven for 25 to 30 minutes, or until the fish flakes easily with a fork.

SERVES 6 · Approximately 280 to 320 calories each serving

Some-Like-It-Hot Salad

- 2 medium-size heads of iceberg lettuce
- 2 chicken bouillon cubes dissolved in 3/4 cup water
- 1 1/2 tablespoons flour
- 1/8 teaspoon ground mace
- Salt and pepper
- 1 medium-size firm tomato, peeled, seeded, and shredded

Quarter the heads of lettuce and put them in a large saucepan with the chicken bouillon. Cover and cook over medium heat for 20 minutes. Drain, reserve the stock, and chop the lettuce fine. Reserve ¾ cup of the stock. In another saucepan, mix the flour and mace. Gradually add the reserved stock and cook over low heat, stirring constantly, until the sauce is thick. Add salt and pepper to taste. Mix the lettuce with the sauce and heat together. Spoon into a serving bowl. Heat the shredded tomato for just a few seconds—it must not cook—and scatter over the lettuce.

SERVES 6 · Approximately 20 to 25 calories each serving

17

Mushroom and Watercress Salad
Grilled Lamb and Peppers en Brochette
Cauliflower Italian Style
Pineapple Strawberry Mold
*(unsweetened canned pineapple, diced,
in a low-calorie strawberry-flavored gelatin)*
*Tea or Coffee with Approved Artificial Sweetener
and Skim Milk*

Mushroom and Watercress Salad

1 bunch of watercress
¾ pound firm mushrooms, uncooked
Low-calorie Italian or Thousand Island salad dressing

Break off and discard heavy watercress stems. Wash the cress in a basin of cold water and shake off the water that clings to it. Place the cress on a towel, roll up, and place in the refrigerator. Cut off the bottoms of the mushroom stems. Slice the stems and caps very thin. Pour over them about 3 tablespoons of the dressing, toss to coat the mushrooms, and let them stand for 1 hour, tossing occasionally. Divide the mushrooms among 6 salad plates and add some of the watercress to each. Serve a small pitcher of additional dressing.

SERVES 6 · Approximately 15 to 20 calories each serving

Grilled Lamb and Peppers en Brochette

- 2¼ pounds leg of lamb, cut into 1- to 1¼-inch cubes
- 2 tablespoons red-wine vinegar
- 1 tablespoon very fine-grated onion
- 2 tablespoons salad oil
- 2 teaspoons honey
- ½ teaspoon dried mint leaves
- ½ teaspoon dried marjoram
- ⅛ teaspoon white pepper
- 1 teaspoon salt
- 2 large green peppers, seeded, stem and pith removed, cut into squares
- 2 large sweet red peppers, seeded, stem and pith removed, cut into squares
- 6 small hot red peppers, optional

Trim any excess fat from the meat. In a bowl combine the vinegar, grated onion, salad oil, honey, mint leaves, marjoram, pepper and salt. Toss with the meat and marinate in the refrigerator for 3 hours or more. Lift out the meat with a slotted spoon. Blanch the pepper squares and hot peppers in boiling salted water for 2 minutes. Drain thoroughly, put into the bowl in which the meat marinated, and toss with any marinade remaining in the bowl.

Thread meat on skewers, alternating the pieces with squares of red or green pepper, and terminating with a small hot pepper if desired. Broil fairly close to the heat either outdoors over coals or in the indoor broiler. Turn the skewers frequently and broil for 15 minutes, or until the lamb is pink in the middle.

SERVES 6 · Approximately 430 to 450 calories each serving

Cauliflower Italian Style

- 1 medium-size head of cauliflower
- 1 medium-size onion, minced
- 2 teaspoons vegetable oil
- 1 cup canned Italian plum tomatoes, pulp only
- 1 small garlic clove, crushed
- ½ teaspoon salt
- ½ teaspoon sugar
- 1 tablespoon grated Parmesan cheese
- 1 tablespoon minced parsley

Separate the cauliflowerets from the heavy center stalk. Discard the stalk. Cook the flowerets, covered, in a small amount of boiling salted water for 8 minutes, or until just barely tender, and drain. Sauté the onion in the oil for 2 to 3 minutes, add the cauliflower, and continue cooking until the onion and the cauliflower are lightly browned. Crush the tomatoes with your hand, and add the garlic, salt and sugar; pour over the cauliflower. Simmer for a minute or two, tossing gently to coat the cauliflower with the sauce, and spoon onto a serving platter. Sprinkle with cheese and parsley and serve immediately.

SERVES 6 · Approximately 35 to 45 calories each serving

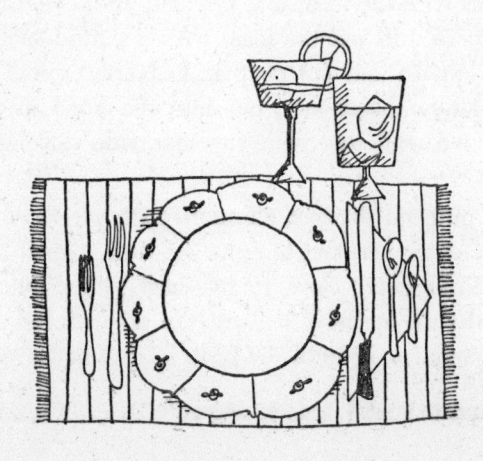

18

Consommé with Egg Slices
Rolled Fillet of Flounder in Tomato Cups
Shortcut Horseradish Ring
Red Delicious Apple with a Small Portion of Dessert Cheese
Tea or Coffee with Approved Artificial Sweetener
and Skim Milk

Consommé with Egg Slices

2 slices of lean bacon, diced
1 large celery rib, diced fine
1 medium-size onion, diced fine
5 cups well-seasoned beef consommé, canned or homemade
3 hard-cooked eggs, cut into slices a scant ¼ inch thick
1 tablespoon minced chives

Sauté the bacon, celery and onion over medium heat until the bacon is almost crisp. Drain off as much of the bacon drippings as possible. Add the beef consommé and simmer, covered, for 30 minutes. Divide the egg slices among 6 soup bowls, and pour in the consommé with the bacon bits and vegetables. Sprinkle with the chives and serve piping hot.

SERVES 6 · Approximately 95 to 105 calories each serving

Rolled Fillet of Flounder in Tomato Cups

3½ pounds fillets of flounder, cut lengthwise into halves
Salt
Dry light wine
6 medium-size firm ripe tomatoes

6 rolled anchovy fillets
1 bunch of watercress, washed and drained, with heavy stems removed
¼ cup low-calorie Italian salad dressing
¼ cup sour cream

Sprinkle each piece of fish generously with salt, roll up, and secure with a food pick. Place the rolls in a small saucepan and fill to a depth of ⅓ inch with wine. Cover and simmer over low heat for 8 or 10 minutes, or until the fish flakes at the touch of a fork. Chill the fish and remove the food picks.

Meanwhile, scald the tomatoes and peel them. Cut off the top and hollow out each one deep enough to hold a roll of fish. Sprinkle the inside of the tomatoes with salt and insert the fish. Top each roll with an anchovy. Place the tomatoes on a platter or on individual plates. Garnish with watercress and refrigerate until serving time. Mix the salad dressing with the sour cream and serve separately.

SERVES 6 · Approximately 235 to 255 calories each serving

Shortcut Horseradish Ring

1 can (12 ounces) mixed vegetable juice
1 envelope (4 servings) low-calorie lemon-flavored gelatin dessert
1 tablespoon lemon juice
Freshly grated or prepared grated horseradish to taste

Heat half of the vegetable juice and dissolve the gelatin in it. Be sure there are no lumps. Add the remaining vegetable juice and the lemon juice. Peel fresh horseradish root before grating enough to flavor the vegetable-juice mixture. If freshly grated horseradish is not available, use the prepared to taste. Pour into a small ring mold or tube pan (about 2 cups) that has been rinsed in cold water. Chill until firm, turn out onto a small platter, and keep refrigerated.

SERVES 6 · Approximately 20 to 25 calories each serving

STARCH

1 Consommé on the Rocks
   * Braised Stuffed Veal Chops 125
   * Zucchini and Potato in Foil 126
   * White Chiffon Layer Cake 126

2 Jellied Beef Consommé
   * Celery-Stuffed Celery 128
   * Baked Bass with Tomatoes and Mushrooms 128
   * Sunshine Cake 129

3 * Baked Potato Miniatures 130
   * Filled Rock Cornish Game Hens, Victorine 131
   * Austrian Sauerkraut 131
   * Orange Cream Sevilla 132

4 Chilled Mixed Vegetable-Juice Cocktail
   * Sesame Slices 133
   * Lamb Leg Aladdin 133
     Tender Young Spinach Salad
   * Hazelnut Torte 134

    (* indicates recipe is given)

DINNERS

5 Romaine Salad Parmigiana
  *Green Noodles with Mussels and Parsley Sauce   135
  Light Italian Bread
  *Pears and Raspberries   136

6 *Swedish Stuffed Cabbage   137
  *Beets and Apples Smitane   138
  New Potatoes
  Scoop of Ice Milk with a Sugar Wafer

7 Cold Artichoke
  *Veal in the Manner of Restaurant Lasserre   139
  *Glazed Onions in Cream   140
  Strawberry Angel Cake

8 *Stuffed Mushrooms Sienna Style   141
  *Linguine with Clam and Tomato Sauce   142
  Dark Italian Bread
  Small Serving of Spumoni or Biscuit Tortoni

(* indicates recipe is given)

9 Lobster Cocktail with Cocktail Sauce
  * Veal and Mushrooms Smitane 143
  * Cucumbers and Pasta Shells 144
  * Pears à la Crème 145

10 Chicken Broth with Pastina
   * Most Elegant Chicken 146
   * Baked Celery with Apples 147
   * Crêpes Soufflés Vert Galant 148

11 * Swiss Geschnetzeltes 149
   * Hungarian Cabbage and Noodles 150
     Beefsteak Tomatoes
   * Scandinavian Meringues 150

12 * Sweetbreads Grand Hôtel de Souillac 151
     Baby Brussels Sprouts
     New Potatoes Cooked in their Jackets
   * Apricot Meringue Noodles 152

13 * South-of-the-Border Pot Roast 153
   * Dutch Mushrooms and Celery 155
     Whipped Potatoes
   * Crêpes à la Mode with Orange Sauce 155

14 * Veal Kidneys Chambertin 156
     Saffron Rice
   * Leeks with Chopped Egg 157
     Chocolate Spongecake

15 * Crisp-Fried Mushrooms 158
   * Bite-Size Meatballs 159
     Green Noodles
   * Vanilla Butter Cake 160

16 Crudités
   * Baked Lobster Stew 161
     New Potatoes Sprinkled with Minced Dill
   * Raspberry Cream Profiteroles 162

17 * Matzoth-Ball Soup 163
   * Norwegian Meat Patties in Cheese Sauce 164
     Baked Tomatoes
   * Oatmeal Rounds 165
     Marble Chiffon

18 * Shrimps Marinara 165
   * Polish Knedle 166
     Boston Lettuce Salad
     Lemon Snowballs

1

Consommé on the Rocks
* Braised Stuffed Veal Chops
* Zucchini and Potato in Foil
* White Chiffon Layer Cake
*Tea or Coffee with Approved Artificial Sweetener
and Skim Milk*

Braised Stuffed Veal Chops

6 loin or rib veal chops, about ¾ inch thick
1 slice of lean bacon, minced
2 large chicken livers
2 tablespoons minced parsley
1 tablespoon minced chives
¼ cup minced celery
2 tablespoons fine bread crumbs
1½ tablespoons oil
2 tablespoons dry vermouth
1 cup chicken stock, or 1 chicken bouillon cube dissolved in 1 cup water
Flour
Skim milk
Salt and pepper

Have the butcher cut a pocket in each of the chops. Sauté the bacon until crisp and remove the pieces from the skillet. Sear the livers in the bacon fat, then chop them into coarse pieces and sauté for 1 minute. Add the parsley, chives and celery, and cook for a few seconds longer. Mix the bacon with the bread crumbs and the chicken-liver mixture. Divide this filling among the chops and secure the openings with food picks. Brown the chops in oil in a large heavy skillet, add the vermouth and chicken stock, and bring to a boil. Reduce the heat and simmer, covered, for 25 to 30 minutes, or until the chops are tender. Remove the chops and keep them warm.

Measure the pan juices. For each cup, blend 1 tablespoon flour with 1 tablespoon skim milk. Add the pan juices, pour back into the skillet and cook, stirring constantly, until thickened. Add salt and pepper to taste. Place the chops on a platter, pour the sauce over them, and serve.

SERVES 6 · Approximately 325 to 375 calories each serving

Zucchini and Potato in Foil

1 large potato, peeled and cut into julienne strips
1½ tablespoons oil
¾ teaspoon salt
Grinding of coarse black pepper
¾ teaspoon dried chervil
¾ teaspoon dried parsley flakes
1 pound tender young zucchini, cut into ¼-inch-thick slices

Parboil the potato for 5 minutes, drain, and cool. Combine the oil, salt, pepper, chervil and parsley flakes in a bowl. Add the potato and zucchini and toss until the vegetables are lightly coated. Place on the center of a large piece of heavy aluminum foil. Fold the foil to make a package and secure tightly. Bake in a preheated 375°F. oven for 25 to 30 minutes, or until the vegetables are tender. Open the foil and bake for an additional 10 minutes.

SERVES 6 · Approximately 50 to 65 calories each serving

White Chiffon Layer Cake

¾ cup flour
½ cup sugar

1 teaspoon baking powder
2 teaspoons grated lemon rind
2 tablespoons butter, melted
2 egg yolks
½ teaspoon vanilla extract
½ teaspoon lemon extract
6 tablespoons water
4 egg whites
¼ teaspoon cream of tartar

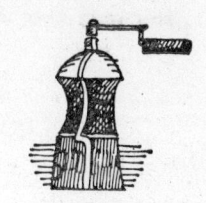

Sift the flour, sugar and baking powder into a bowl; add half of the lemon rind. Make a well in the center of the mixture and pour the butter, egg yolks, vanilla and lemon extracts, and the water into the well. Mix all the ingredients until well blended and smooth. Beat the egg whites until foamy, add the cream of tartar, and beat until very stiff. Quickly fold into the batter and pour into two well-greased 8-inch layer-cake pans. Bake in a preheated 325°F. oven for 30 minutes. Invert the pans onto a rack. When the layers are cool, spread the frosting between them and on the top sides of the cake. Sprinkle remaining lemon rind on top.

White Frosting

1 egg white
3 tablespoons sugar
2 tablespoons corn syrup
1 tablespoon water
½ teaspoon lemon extract

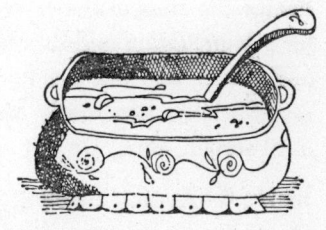

Beat the egg white until stiff. Put the sugar, corn syrup, and 1 tablespoon water into a small saucepan. Boil together until the syrup spins a thread, then pour over the beaten egg white, beating constantly until thick and glossy. Beat in the lemon extract.

SERVES 6 to 8 · Approximately 190 to 250 calories each serving

Note: To facilitate removing the baked layers from the pans, line the bottoms, after greasing, with wax-paper circles cut to fit. After removing the layers, peel off the wax paper.

2

Jellied Beef Consommé
* Celery-Stuffed Celery
* Baked Bass wtih Tomatoes and Mushrooms
* Sunshine Cake
*Tea or Coffee with Approved Artificial Sweetener
and Skim Milk*

Celery-Stuffed Celery

12 wide pieces of celery, 3 to 3½ inches long
⅔ cup small-curd cottage cheese
⅓ cup very fine-minced celery
1 tablespoon minced chives
Lawry's Seasoned Salt

Fringe the ends of the celery with a knife, and crisp in ice water for 1 hour. Drain and dry. Mix the cottage cheese, minced celery and chives, and put a mound on the center of each piece of celery. Sprinkle generously with seasoned salt. Keep refrigerated until serving time. Do not assemble more than an hour ahead.

SERVES 6 · Approximately 35 to 40 calories each serving

Baked Bass with Tomatoes and Mushrooms

4-pound bass, filleted
½ teaspoon seasoned salt
Grinding of coarse black pepper

3 scallions, including some of the green part, sliced fine
1 tablespoon oil
⅓ pound mushrooms, sliced thin
1½ cups canned Italian plum tomatoes
¼ cup dry vermouth
1 teaspoon Escoffier Sauce Robert
2 tablespoons fine bread crumbs

Place the fillets, side by side and skin side down, in a lightly greased shallow oven-to-table baking dish. Sprinkle the fish with half of the seasoned salt and a little pepper; bake, uncovered, in a preheated 375°F. oven for 30 minutes.

Meanwhile, prepare the sauce: Sauté the scallions in half of the oil until golden, add the mushrooms, and sauté for 1 minute longer. Add the remaining ingredients except the bread crumbs, and spoon over the partially baked fish. Mix the bread crumbs with the remaining oil and sprinkle over the fish. Bake for an additional 20 minutes, or until the fish flakes easily when tested with a fork.

SERVES 6 · Approximately 350 to 400 calories each serving

Sunshine Cake

6 eggs, separated
½ cup plus 1 tablespoon sugar
Grated rind and juice of 1 small orange
3 tablespoons potato starch
3 tablespoons cake flour
Confectioners' sugar

Beat the egg whites until stiff but not dry. Beat the egg yolks lightly and then gradually beat in the sugar and continue to beat until thick and light. Stir in the orange rind and juice. Sift the potato starch and cake flour together, and mix lightly into the batter. Fold in the stiffly beaten egg whites. Pour into an ungreased 9- or 10-inch tube pan. Bake in a preheated 325°F. oven for 45 to 50 minutes, or until the top springs back when pressed lightly. Invert the pan on a cake rack and let the cake cool completely before removing it from the pan. Dust lightly with confectioners' sugar.

SERVES 6 to 8 · Approximately 135 to 175 calories (135 calories each serving for an 8-serving cake, 175 calories each serving for a 6-serving cake)

3

Baked Potato Miniatures
Filled Rock Cornish Game Hens, Victorine
Austrian Sauerkraut
Orange Cream Sevilla
Tea or Coffee with Approved Artificial Sweetener
and Skim Milk

Baked Potato Miniatures

6 small new potatoes
Vegetable oil
2 tablespoons sour cream
1 teaspoon minced chives
Salt

Scrub the potatoes, dry them, and rub the surface with a little oil. Make a small slit in the skin of each potato, and bake in a preheated 400°F. oven for 30 to 40 minutes, or until soft. Combine the sour cream and chives, and season with salt. Cut the baked potatoes into halves, place a dab of the sour-cream mixture on top of each potato half, and serve immediately.

SERVES 6 · Approximately 35 to 45 calories each serving

Filled Rock Cornish Game Hens, Victorine

1 red onion, minced
1 large celery rib, minced
2 teaspoons butter
3 chicken livers
1 large firm apple, peeled and diced
3 tablespoons low-calorie orange marmalade
2 cups cooked broad noodles, chopped
Salt and pepper
6 small individual-size Rock Cornish Game hens
1 tablespoon melted butter

Sauté the onion and celery in 2 teaspoons butter, covered, for 5 minutes. Uncover, add the livers, and cook just until they lose their pink color. Chop the livers into coarse pieces. Add the apple, marmalade and noodles, mix all together, and season with salt and pepper. Stuff the game hens with the mixture, skewer the vents, and place side by side in a roasting pan. Brush lightly with the melted butter. Roast in a preheated 450°F. oven for 10 minutes, reduce the heat to 375°F., cover, and roast for 20 minutes. Then uncover once more and roast until the game hens are tender.

SERVES 6 · Approximately 390 to 415 calories each serving

Austrian Sauerkraut

3 slices (each ½ inch thick) Polish or Hungarian sausage
2 pounds sauerkraut, rinsed under cold water and drained
2 cups beef consommé, or 2 beef bouillon cubes dissolved in 2 cups water
1 small apple, grated
2 whole cloves
4 peppercorns
1 bay leaf
Salt

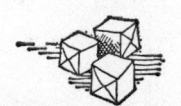

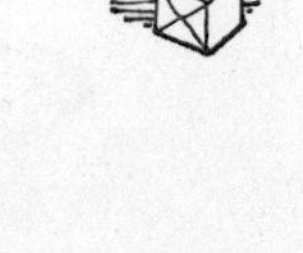

Skin the sausage and cut into small dice. Cook it slowly in a heavy-bottomed saucepan until it begins to brown in its own fat. Add the sauerkraut, consommé and apple. Tie the cloves, peppercorns and bay leaf in a small cheesecloth bag, add to the sauerkraut and cook, covered, over low heat for 1 hour. Discard the bag of spices, and add salt to taste.

SERVES 6 · Approximately 45 to 55 calories each serving

Orange Cream Sevilla

3 eggs, separated
3 cups skim milk
1½ envelopes (4 servings per envelope) low-calorie orange-flavored gelatin dessert
½ cup low-calorie whipped topping
1 can (11 ounces) mandarin oranges, very well drained

Place the egg yolks in a small saucepan, beat lightly, and add the milk and gelatin. Cook over low heat, stirring constantly, until the gelatin dissolves and the custard coats the spoon. Remove from the heat, cool, and chill. When the mixture is on the point of setting, beat the egg whites until stiff but not dry and fold into the custard. Spoon the pudding into 6 dessert dishes. Chill in the refrigerator until set. Before serving top each portion with a little of the whipped topping and garnish with mandarin-orange sections.

SERVES 6 · Approximately 135 to 145 calories each serving

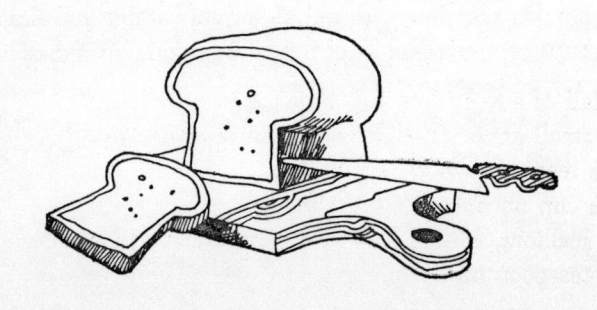

4

Chilled Mixed Vegetable-Juice Cocktail
* Sesame Slices
* Lamb Leg Aladdin
Tender Young Spinach Salad (Discard any heavy stems, crips in the refrigerator, toss with low-calorie dressing.)
* Hazelnut Torte
Tea or Coffee with Approved Artificial Sweetener and Skim Milk

Sesame Slices

2 slices of firm-textured buttermilk rye bread
2 teaspoons sweet butter
1 tablespoon sesame seeds

Trim the crusts from the bread. Spread the slices with butter and sprinkle with seeds. Cut each piece into 3 fingers and place them on a baking sheet. Bake in a preheated 325°F. oven for 25 minutes.

MAKES 6 slices • Approximately 28 calories each slice

Lamb Leg Aladdin

Half of a 5- to 6-pound leg of lamb
1 small garlic clove, mashed with 1 teaspoon salt
⅛ teaspoon white pepper
¼ cup uncooked brown rice
3 scallions, with a little of the green part, sliced fine
1 teaspoon oil

1 cup fresh spinach leaves, chopped into coarse pieces
¼ cup shelled young peas
2 tablespoons minced parsley
Salt
1 onion, sliced
½ cup water

Have the butcher bone the lamb and cut a pocket in it. Rub the garlic mixture on the meat, inside and out. Sprinkle with white pepper.

Cook the rice according to package directions until it is just tender. Sauté the scallions in the oil for 5 minutes. Add the spinach leaves and cook for a few seconds longer. Remove from the heat and add to the cooked rice. Stir in the peas and parsley. Add salt to taste and spoon into the lamb pocket. Close the opening and secure with skewers or string. Place in a small shallow roasting pan, add the onion and water, and roast in a preheated 400°F. oven for 1¼ hours, or until tender. Baste frequently and add more water if the liquid evaporates. Remove the skewers or string, slice the meat, and place on a serving platter. Skim any fat from the pan juices and spoon the juices over the meat.

SERVES 6 or more · Approximately 400 to 475 calories each serving of 2 slices

Hazelnut Torte

3 eggs, separated
⅓ cup sugar
2 tablespoons light rum
½ teaspoon almond extract
½ cup ground hazelnuts
3 tablespoons ground almonds
Fine dry bread crumbs
½ cup Cool Whip or other low-calorie whipped topping

Beat the egg whites until they form moist peaks and gradually beat in half of the sugar. Beat the meringue until it is very stiff.

Beat the egg yolks with the remaining sugar until the mixture is very thick and light, and beat in the rum and almond extract. Gently fold the meringue into the egg yolks and add the ground hazelnuts and almonds. Pour into a very well-buttered 9-inch tube pan that has been dusted with bread crumbs. Bake in a preheated 325°F. oven for 30 minutes, or until the top of the cake springs back when pressed gently. Cool on a rack. At serving time, cut into 6 portions, and top each portion with some of the topping.

SERVES 6 · Approximately 160 to 185 calories each serving

Note: It is not always easy to remove a nut torte from the tin. For an easier method, butter the pan but do *not* sprinkle it with bread crumbs. Instead, line the bottom of the tin with wax paper cut to fit, and butter the paper before pouring in the batter. After the cake has cooled, run a sharp knife around the tin, turn the cake out, and peel off the paper.

5

Romaine Salad Parmigiana (young romaine, dressed with low-calorie Italian dressing, sprinkled with Parmesan cheese)
* *Green Noodles with Mussels and Parsley Sauce*
Light Italian Bread (Allow 1 or 2 small slices for each person.)
* *Pears and Raspberries*
Tea or Coffee with Approved Artificial Sweetener and Skim Milk

Green Noodles with Mussels and Parsley Sauce

36 large to 48 medium-size mussels in shells
½ cup dry white wine

3 scallions, white part only, sliced thin
1 tablespoon olive oil
1 tablespoon flour
⅓ cup minced parsley
Salt and pepper
¾ pound green noodles

Scrub the mussels and remove as much beard as possible with a small sharp knife. Put the mussels in a soup kettle or Dutch oven. Pour in the wine and cook, covered, over high heat for 6 to 8 minutes, or until the shells open. Discard any mussels that have not opened. Remove the mussels, discard the shells, and keep the mussels warm. Strain the liquor through a cloth-lined sieve and reserve ¾ cup.

In the same kettle or Dutch oven sauté the scallions in the oil for 5 minutes, stirring frequently. Blend in the flour and add the reserved liquor gradually, stirring constantly, until the sauce thickens. Add the parsley, and salt and pepper to taste. Meanwhile, cook the noodles according to package directions. Rinse under hot water and drain thoroughly. Add the mussels to the sauce and heat, but do not cook any longer. Pour over the noodles, toss gently, and serve piping hot.

SERVES 6 · Approximately 340 to 365 calories each serving

Pears and Raspberries

3 tablespoons sugar
¼ cup water
1-inch piece of vanilla bean, slit on one side
6 medium-size pears, peeled, cored, and cut into halves
2 cups raspberries
2½ tablespoons currant jelly, melted and cooled

Bring sugar and water to a boil. Turn heat low. Add vanilla bean and pear halves. (The fruit will release liquid to make enough syrup.) Cover and simmer for 7 minutes, or until the pears are just tender. Cool the fruit and drain it well. Mix the berries very gently with the jelly. Mound on the pear halves. Arrange the fruit on a serving platter, or place 2 halves on each dessert plate.

SERVES 6 · Approximately 140 to 155 calories each serving

6

Swedish Stuffed Cabbage
Beets and Apples Smitane
New Potatoes (Peel a thin strip around the middle of each potato before cooking. Allow 1 or 2 potatoes for each serving.)
Scoop of Ice Milk with a Sugar Wafer
Tea or Coffee with Approved Artificial Sweetener and Skim Milk

Swedish Stuffed Cabbage

3-pound head of cabbage (Choose one with large leaves.)
½ pound lean veal
½ pound lean beef
¼ pound lean pork
1 egg, lightly beaten
1½ cups cooked rice
½ teaspoon grated nutmeg
⅛ teaspoon white pepper
1 teaspoon salt
1½ tablespoons bacon drippings
2 beef bouillon cubes dissolved in 1½ cups water

Cut out and discard the core of the cabbage. Cook the cabbage in boiling salted water until the leaves separate easily. Drain, set aside 12 large or 18 medium-size leaves, and chop the balance of the cabbage into coarse pieces.

Have the butcher grind the veal, beef and pork together. Place the meat in a mixing bowl and add the egg, rice, nutmeg, pepper and salt. With your hands, mix until smooth. Add more seasoning if desired. Trim the thick center rib of the reserved cabbage leaves, and put a portion of the meat filling on each leaf. Fold the sides of the leaves over the filling, then roll up to enclose the filling completely.

Melt a little of the bacon drippings in a heavy skillet, brown the chopped cabbage in the drippings, and spread it over the bottom of a shallow roasting pan that can accommodate the cabbage rolls in a single layer. In the same skillet, melt the remaining drippings, brown the cabbage rolls on all sides, and arrange them on the bed of cabbage. Add more drippings, if needed. Add the beef bouillon, cover the roasting pan, and bake in a preheated 325°F. oven for 1¾ hours. Add more bouillon if necessary to keep the cabbage rolls moistened until they are done.

SERVES 6 · Approximately 300 to 325 calories each serving

Beets and Apples Smitane

6 medium-size beets, peeled
2 medium-size apples, peeled and cored
2 teaspoons lemon juice
1 teaspoon sugar
Salt
1 tablespoon flour
2 tablespoons sour cream
Dash of white pepper

Grate the beets and apples, using the coarse side of the grater, into a heavy saucepan. Add the lemon juice, sugar, and ½ teaspoon salt. Simmer the mixture over low heat for 20 minutes, or until the beets and apples are tender. Mix the flour with the sour cream, add to the beet mixture, and simmer for 3 or 4 minutes, stirring constantly. Add the pepper, and more salt to taste.

SERVES 6 · Approximately 65 to 80 calories each serving

7

*Cold Artichoke (1 small artichoke for each serving; use
low-calorie salad dressing as dip.)*
* Veal in the Manner of Restaurant Lasserre
* Glazed Onions in Cream
*Strawberry Angel Cake (1 small slice for each serving,
with crushed strawberry sauce)*
*Tea or Coffee with Approved Artificial Sweetener
and Skim Milk*

Veal in the Manner of Restaurant Lasserre

6 crêpes
1 tablespoon oil
4 tablespoons butter
6 pieces of veal cutlet, ⅓ inch thick, each weighing about ¼ pound
¾ teaspoon salt
⅛ teaspoon white pepper
½ pound mushrooms, minced
4 shallots, peeled and minced
½ teaspoon Lawry's Seasoned Salt
¼ cup dry sherry
¼ cup grated Swiss cheese

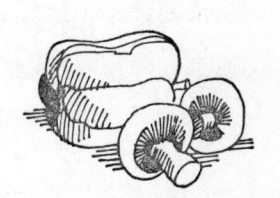

Make 6 crêpes according to directions in Basic Crêpes (see Index). In a heavy skillet, melt the oil and 1 tablespoon of the butter over medium-high heat. Brown the meat quickly on both sides, reduce the heat to medium, and continue cooking for 2 minutes on each side, or until the meat is cooked through but not dry. Remove the meat, sprinkle with salt and pepper, and set aside. Melt an additional tablespoon of butter in the skillet.

Add the mushrooms and shallots and cook, stirring constantly, for about 4 minutes, or until almost all the liquid has evaporated. Add the seasoned salt and sherry. Spread a portion of this mushroom *duxelles* on the center of each crêpe, place a slice of veal on top, and cover with the remaining *duxelles*. Fold over the sides of the crêpes, and place them side by side and seam side down in a single layer in a shallow ovenproof dish that can come to the table. Scatter the cheese over the crêpes and dot with the remaining butter. Bake in a preheated 450°F. oven for 10 to 15 minutes, or until the cheese is bubbling and golden.

SERVES 6 · Approximately 300 to 325 calories each serving

Glazed Onions in Cream

- 1 pound small white onions, peeled
- 2 teaspoons butter
- 2 teaspoons sugar
- 1 chicken bouillon cube dissolved in ½ cup water
- 1 tablespoon heavy cream

In a heavy skillet, brown the onions in the butter and sugar, shaking the pan constantly to brown the onions evenly. Add the chicken bouillon and cook the onions, covered, for 30 minutes, or until they are tender. Remove from the heat, stir in the cream, adjust seasonings, and serve.

SERVES 6 · Approximately 55 to 65 calories each serving

8

* *Stuffed Mushrooms Sienna Style*
* *Linguine with Clam and Tomato Sauce*
Dark Italian Bread (Allow 1 or 2 small slices for each person.)
Small Serving of Spumoni or Biscuit Tortoni
Tea or Coffee with Approved Artificial Sweetener and Skim Milk

~~~

Stuffed Mushrooms Sienna Style

1 large red onion, minced
1 tablespoon vegetable oil
24 large mushrooms
2 tablespoons minced parsley
2 tablespoons minced prosciutto
2 tablespoons pine nuts
Coarse black pepper
Salt

Sauté the onion in the oil until the onion is translucent. Remove the stems of the mushrooms and mince them. Add to the cooked onions with the parsley, prosciutto, nuts, and pepper and salt to taste. Divide the filling among the mushroom caps, place them in a covered shallow baking dish, and bake them in a preheated 400°F. oven for 15 minutes, or until done.

SERVES 6 · Approximately 45 to 55 calories each serving

Linguine with Clam and Tomato Sauce

1 medium-size onion, minced
1 tablespoon olive oil
3 tablespoons capers, drained
1 pound fresh tomatoes, peeled, seeded, and chopped
2 cans (7½ ounces each) chopped clams
Salt
Coarse black pepper
1 pound linguine, cooked *al dente,* according to package directions
¼ cup minced parsley
Freshly grated Parmesan cheese

In a heavy saucepan, sauté the onion in the oil until the onion is golden. Add the capers and tomatoes and simmer, covered, for 30 minutes. Stir in the clams, and salt and pepper to taste. Mix the sauce with the hot linguine. Sprinkle the parsley on top. Serve the cheese separately.

SERVES 6 · Approximately 325 to 345 calories each serving

9

Lobster Cocktail with Cocktail Sauce
* *Veal and Mushrooms Smitane*
* *Cucumbers and Pasta Shells*
* *Pears à la Crème*
Tea or Coffee with Approved Artificial Sweetener and Skim Milk

Veal and Mushrooms Smitane

1 pound fresh mushrooms, quartered
4 teaspoons butter
2 tablespoons lemon juice
1 teaspoon Italian seasoning
Salt
¼ teaspoon garlic salt
⅛ teaspoon coarse black pepper
1 tablespoon oil
2 pounds veal cutlet, ⅓ to ½ inch thick, cut into julienne strips
2 eggs, beaten
1 tablespoon soy sauce
2 slices of soft white bread, torn into pieces
1 small onion, grated
1½ pounds leg of veal, ground
2 chicken bouillon cubes dissolved in 1 cup water
3 tablespoons flour
2 tablespoons catsup
3 tablespoons sour cream

Place the mushrooms in a saucepan with 1 teaspoon of the butter, the lemon juice, Italian seasoning, ½ teaspoon salt, the garlic salt and black pepper. Cover and simmer over the low heat for 5 minutes. Drain, reserve the juices, and transfer the mushrooms to a shallow oven-to-table baking dish. Melt 2 teaspoons of the butter in a large heavy skillet, add half of the oil, and sauté the veal strips, half at a time, until they just begin to render their juices. Add the juices to the mushroom juice, and scatter the meat over the mushrooms in the baking dish.

Make the meatballs: Combine the eggs, soy sauce, bread and grated onion. Mash to a paste, mix thoroughly with the ground veal, and add salt to taste. Shape into meatballs. Melt the remaining teaspoon of butter in the heavy skillet and add the remaining oil. Brown the meatballs quickly over high heat and scatter them in the baking dish. Deglaze the skillet with the bouillon cubes dissolved in water, and add to the reserved juices.

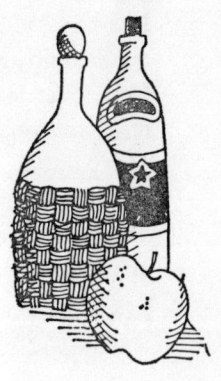

Mix the flour, catsup and sour cream in the skillet. Add the accumulated juices gradually and stir with a whisk until smooth. Cook over low heat, stirring constantly, until the sauce is thickened and smooth. If the sauce is too thick, add a bit more water. (Preparation up to this point may be done in advance.) To finish, pour the sauce over the meat and mushrooms in the baking dish, and bake in a preheated 350°F. oven for 25 to 30 minutes, or until bubbling.

SERVES 8 · Approximately 425 to 475 calories each serving

Cucumbers and Pasta Shells

3 large cucumbers, peeled, seeded, and cut into bite-size pieces
1½ teaspoons chicken concentrate, or 2 chicken bouillon cubes, crushed
¼ pound pasta shells
¾ teaspoon dried chervil
Salt and pepper

Place the cucumbers and the chicken concentrate in a saucepan. Cover and cook over medium heat, stirring occasionally, until the cucumbers are tender. Raise the heat, uncover the saucepan, and boil, if necessary, to reduce the liquid to 2 tablespoons.

Meanwhile, cook the pasta shells according to package directions. Drain, toss with the cucumbers, then add the chervil, and salt and pepper to taste.

SERVES 6 · Approximately 75 to 90 calories each serving

Pears à la Crème

2 large firm pears
⅓ cup dark brown sugar
2 tablespoons granulated sugar
¼ cup unsweetened pineapple juice
1 cup Cool Whip or other low-calorie whipped topping

Peel and core the pears and cut them into large dice. Place them in a saucepan with the dark brown sugar, granulated sugar, and the pineapple juice. Bring to a boil, stirring until the sugar dissolves. Reduce the heat to medium, cover, and cook until the fruit is just tender. Uncover and cook over high heat until the juices become syrupy and thick. Remove from the heat and cool. Chill until serving time. Fold in topping at the last moment and serve.

SERVES 6 • Approximately 140 to 155 calories each serving

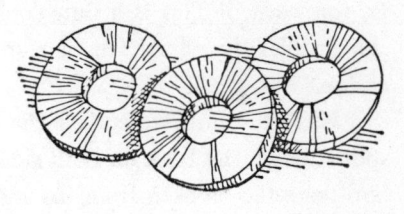

10

Chicken Broth with Pastina (Add pastina to strained broth
and cook for a few minutes.)
* *Most Elegant Chicken*
* *Baked Celery with Apples*
* *Crêpes Soufflés Vert Galant*
*Tea or Coffee with Approved Artificial Sweetener
and Skim Milk*

Most Elegant Chicken

3½-pound fryer or broiler chicken
1¼ cups chicken consommé, or 2 chicken bouillon cubes dissolved in 1¼ cups water
1 sweetbread, about ¾ pound
3 scallions, white part only, sliced fine
1 teaspoon butter
1 egg, lightly beaten
1 slice of white bread, crumbled to fine pieces
½ cup minced mushrooms, sautéed in 1 teaspoon butter
2 tablespoons minced cooked ham
1 tablespoon truffle peelings or minced truffles
2 tablespoons port
Salt and pepper
2 teaspoons cornstarch

Be forewarned! This is a time-consuming recipe but the end result justifies the effort. This is a splendid dish worthy of any occasion.

Have the butcher cut off the wing tips of the chicken and split it down the back on both sides of the backbone. Then have him bone the chicken from the inside, except for the leg bones, taking care not to tear the skin.

Place all the chicken bones in a saucepan, add the consommé and simmer, covered, for 1 hour. There should be about 1 cup stock. Strain it and reserve.

Parboil the sweetbread in water to cover for 15 minutes, plunge into ice water for 10 minutes, then trim off as much membrane and connective tissue as possible and cut the meat into fine dice. Cut the chicken liver into quarters and sauté it with the scallions in 1 teaspoon butter. Chop them together into fine pieces.

Combine the egg, bread, mushrooms, ham, truffle, half of the port, the sweetbread, and the scallion-liver mixture. Add salt and pepper to taste.

Lay the chicken skin side down on a board, sprinkle lightly with salt, and put the filling down the center of the bird. Fold the chicken to enclose the filling and secure with small skewers. Roast the chicken in a preheated 450°F. oven for 15 minutes, reduce the heat to 400°F., and roast for 35 minutes longer, or until tender. Transfer the chicken to a serving platter and keep warm.

Deglaze the roasting pan with the reserved stock. Mix the cornstarch with the remaining port mixed with 1 tablespoon cold water. Add to the pan and cook, stirring constantly, until the sauce is thickened and clear. Cut the chicken crosswise into slices about ¾ inch thick. Serve the sauce separately in a sauceboat.

SERVES 6 · Approximately 300 to 350 calories each serving

Baked Celery with Apples

3 heads of celery
Chicken stock, or chicken bouillon cubes dissolved in water
2 medium-size apples
1 tablespoon butter
2 teaspoons sugar

Cut the celery about 7 inches long from the root end. Trim the heads, and cut them lengthwise into halves. Put them in a shallow baking dish, and add chicken stock to a depth of ¾ inch. Cover and bake in a preheated 375°F. oven for 1 hour, or until the celery is tender.

Meanwhile, peel, core, and slice the apples. Sauté them in the butter over high heat until they are lightly browned. Place the apple slices in a row on each head of celery, sprinkle with the sugar, and bake the dish, uncovered, for 30 minutes longer, basting frequently with the stock.

SERVES 6 · Approximately 55 to 65 calories each serving

Crêpes Soufflés Vert Galant

1 recipe Basic Crêpes (see Index)
2½ tablespoons flour
2½ tablespoons sugar
⅛ teaspoon salt
¾ cup milk
3 eggs, separated
½ teaspoon vanilla extract
Confectioners' sugar
Grand Marnier

Spread the 6 crêpes on a board or working surface, speckled side up. Mix the flour, sugar and salt in a saucepan. Gradually add the milk and cook over low heat, stirring constantly, until thick. Remove from the heat, mix in the egg yolks, and replace over the heat for a minute or so, until the mixture is just about to boil. Remove from the heat again and stir in the vanilla. (Preparation up to this point may be done in advance.)

Shortly before serving time, beat the egg whites until stiff but not dry and fold them into the custard. Spoon a portion of this soufflé mixture down the center of each crêpe, roll the crêpes up very loosely, and place them seam side down on a well-buttered baking sheet. Bake them in a preheated 400°F. oven for about 5 minutes so that the soufflé remains creamy and the crêpes do not dry out. With the help of 2 broad spatulas or pancake turners, transfer the crêpes to individual plates and dust them generously with confectioners' sugar. Serve immediately, accompanied by a bottle of Grand Marnier so that each guest may pour some of the liqueur over his crêpe.

SERVES 6 · Approximately 130 to 150 calories each serving

Note: Crêpes may be baked and served in individual shallow ovenproof dishes.

11

Swiss Geschnetzeltes
Hungarian Cabbage and Noodles
Beefsteak Tomatoes (thick slices, sprinkled with basil)
Scandinavian Meringues
Tea or Coffee with Approved Artificial Sweetener
and Skim Milk

Swiss Geschnetzeltes

- 2¼ pounds very tender veal (fillet, preferably), sliced ⅓ inch thick
- 1 tablespoon butter
- 1 tablespoon vegetable oil
- 2 cans (8 ounces each) mushrooms
- 1 large onion, minced
- ⅓ cup dry vermouth
- ¼ cup sour cream
- 1 tablespoon flour
- Salt
- White pepper
- ¼ cup minced parsley

Cut the veal into strips ½ inch wide. Melt the butter with the oil in a large heavy skillet. Add the veal, a portion at a time, and sauté over medium-high heat until the meat turns white. Remove the veal with a slotted spoon and set aside. (If you notice that the meat is rendering its juices, remove it immediately. The meat must not overcook lest it become tough and dry.) When all the veal has been seared, drain the mushrooms, reserve the juice, and add the mushrooms to the skillet with the onion. Cook for 2 minutes. Add the vermouth and the mushroom juice to the sour cream that has been mixed with the flour. Pour over the mushroom-onion mixture and cook over medium heat, stirring constantly, until the sauce thickens. Add the reserved veal and heat but do not allow to cook. Add salt and pepper to taste. Pour into a serving bowl, sprinkle with parsley, and serve at once.

SERVES 6 · Approximately 360 to 385 calories each serving

Hungarian Cabbage and Noodles

- 1 medium-size head of cabbage
- 1 tablespoon sugar
- 1 tablespoon rendered bacon fat
- 1 teaspoon salt
- ¼ teaspoon white pepper
- ¼ pound medium-wide noodles

Quarter the cabbage, cut out the core, and shred the balance. In a heavy iron skillet or Dutch oven, caramelize the sugar. Add the bacon fat, salt and pepper. Mix, then add the cabbage and toss with the other ingredients. Cover and cook over low heat for 1 hour, or until it is tender, stirring constantly. Shortly before the cabbage is finished, boil the noodles according to package directions. Combine the cabbage and noodles, heat together until piping hot, and serve immediately.

SERVES 6 · Approximately 125 to 140 calories each serving

Scandinavian Meringues

- 1 egg white
- ¼ cup sugar
- 1 teaspoon potato starch
- ⅛ teaspoon pulverized ammonium carbonate (Available in drugstores; keep it tightly capped against evaporation.)

Beat the egg white until it forms moist peaks. Gradually add the sugar, beating constantly until the sugar is dissolved and the mixture is thick and glossy. Sift the potato starch with the ammonium carbonate and fold into the meringue. With a teaspoon, drop 16 to 20 mounds of meringue 1½ inches apart on a buttered cooky sheet. Bake for 20 minutes in a preheated 200°F. oven, turn off the heat, and leave in the oven for 1 hour to dry out.

MAKES 16 to 20 meringues · Approximately 11 to 14 calories each meringue

12

Sweetbreads Grand Hôtel de Souillac
Baby Brussels Sprouts
New Potatoes Cooked in their Jackets
**Apricot Meringue Noodles*
Tea or Coffee with Approved Artificial Sweetener and Skim Milk

Sweetbreads Grand Hôtel de Souillac

3 to 3½ pounds untrimmed veal sweetbreads
1 tablespoon vinegar
1 cup minced onions
1 cup minced carrots
4 tablespoons butter
¾ teaspoon salt
¼ teaspoon white pepper
¼ teaspoon ground thyme
2 tablespoons flour
¾ cup water
½ teaspoon meat extract
2 tablespoons port
2 tablespoons minced truffles

Soak the sweetbreads in 1 quart water mixed with the vinegar for 30 minutes; drain. Parboil the sweetbreads in salted water for 10 minutes. Transfer them to ice water for an additional 10 minutes, then remove the sweetbreads. Discard the pipes and connective tissues and slice the sweetbreads.

In a large shallow heatproof casserole, over low heat, sauté the onions and carrots in 3 tablespoons of the butter for 5 minutes, stirring frequently. Place the sweetbreads in a single layer over the vegetables and sprinkle with salt, pepper and thyme. Cover and place in a preheated 325°F. oven for 30 minutes. Drain off the pan juices and reserve them.

In a saucepan over medium heat melt the remaining tablespoon of butter. Blend in the flour and gradually add the reserved pan juices and the ¾ cup water. Cook until the sauce thickens. Stir in the meat extract, wine and truffles. Pour over the sweetbreads, cover, and simmer together for 15 minutes. Serve immediately.

SERVES 6 · Approximately 240 to 265 calories each serving

Apricot Meringue Noodles

1 recipe Sweet Crêpes (see below)
½ cup dried apricot halves, minced
3 egg whites
6 tablespoons sugar

Cool the crêpes and cut them into broad "noodles." Toss them lightly and place in a well-buttered 9- or 10-inch oven-to-table baking dish. Sprinkle the minced apricots on top. About 30 minutes or less before serving time, beat the egg whites until foamy. Add the sugar gradually, beating constantly, until the meringue is stiff and shiny. Spread over the apricots and bake in a preheated 325°F. oven for 12 minutes, or until light brown. Serve immediately.

SERVES 6 · Approximately 190 to 210 calories each serving

Sweet Crêpes

1 egg
½ cup flour
2 tablespoons sugar
¼ teaspoon salt
¾ cup milk
1 tablespoon melted butter

Beat the egg with a whisk, add half of the flour, and beat until smooth. Add the sugar, salt, and half of the milk, stirring again until smooth. Beat in the remaining flour and milk.

Follow the method of frying crêpes in the Basic Crêpes recipe (see Index), using the melted butter. Fry as many crêpes in a heavy 8-inch pan as the batter will yield. You should have 8 or 9.

Approximately 55 to 65 calories each crêpe

13

* South-of-the-Border Pot Roast
* Dutch Mushrooms and Celery
Whipped Potatoes (small portion; add hot skim milk instead of butter)
* Crêpes à la Mode with Orange Sauce
Tea or Coffee with Approved Artificial Sweetener and Skim Milk

South-of-the-Border Pot Roast

2½ pounds beef bottom round
½ tablespoon oil
1 large onion, sliced

1 garlic clove, mashed
1 teaspoon salt
1 teaspoon ground cinnamon
1 tablespoon vinegar
1 tablespoon catsup
2 cups water
4 whole cloves
1 bay leaf
½ ounce unsweetened chocolate

In a Dutch oven, brown the meat in the oil, turning it to sear on all sides. Remove the meat and set aside. Sauté the onion in the same pan until the slices are golden. Replace the meat. Combine the garlic, salt, cinnamon, vinegar, catsup and water and pour over the meat. Tie the cloves and bay leaf in a small piece of cheesecloth and add to the pot. Cover the Dutch oven and roast in a preheated 375°F. oven for 2½ hours, or until the meat is tender.

Remove the meat from the pot. Discard the cloves and bay leaf. Place the juices in a freezer so that the fat will rise quickly and can be skimmed off. Add the chocolate to the pan juices and cook over low heat, stirring constantly, until the chocolate melts. Adjust the seasoning. Cut the meat into ⅓-inch-thick slices and arrange the slices in a shallow ovenproof dish, preferably one that can come to the table. Pour the sauce over the meat, cover, and refrigerate until shortly before serving time. Reheat in the oven.

SERVES 6 · Approximately 360 to 420 calories each serving

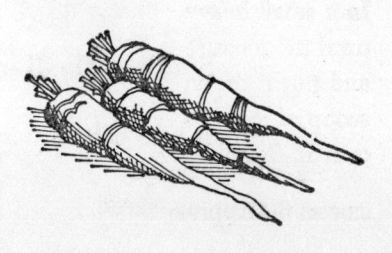

Dutch Mushrooms and Celery

2 cans (4 ounces each) whole mushrooms
4 cups diced celery
2 tablespoons butter
¼ teaspoon beef concentrate
2 tablespoons Holland gin
2 tablespoons lemon juice
1 teaspoon sugar
Dash of white pepper
½ teaspoon salt

Drain the mushrooms and reserve the juice. Sauté the mushrooms and celery in the butter for 5 minutes, stirring frequently. Transfer to a casserole. Combine the remaining ingredients with the reserved juice and pour over the sautéed vegetables. Bake, covered, in a preheated 375°F. oven for 1 hour.

SERVES 6 · Approximately 55 to 65 calories each serving

Crêpes à la Mode with Orange Sauce

1 tablespoon butter
2 tablespoons sugar
⅓ cup orange juice
6 crêpes (Gossamer Crêpes, see Index)
1 pint vanilla ice milk
2 tablespoons grated orange rind

In a small heavy skillet, cook the butter, sugar and orange juice until the mixture is lightly syrupy. Bathe each crêpe in the sauce and put it on an individual plate. Work quickly. Place a ⅓-cup scoop of ice milk on each crêpe, and spoon any remaining syrup over it. Sprinkle orange rind on top and serve immediately.

SERVES 6 · Approximately 135 to 145 calories each serving

14

Veal Kidneys Chambertin
Saffron Rice (Use low-calorie rice; allow small portions.)
Leeks with Chopped Egg
Chocolate Spongecake (Substitute cocoa for part of the flour in an ordinary light sponge.)
Tea or Coffee with Approved Artificial Sweetener and Skim Milk

Veal Kidneys Chambertin

1 tablespoon butter
¼ cup minced shallots
1 large carrot, minced
1 large onion, minced
6 veal kidneys
2 chicken bouillon cubes dissolved in 1½ cups water
¾ cup Burgundy wine
¾ teaspoon salt
Pinch of white pepper
3 tablespoons evaporated milk, undiluted
1 teaspoon Dijon mustard

Melt the butter in a heavy skillet or saucepan. Add the shallots, carrot and onion, and sauté over medium heat for 5 minutes. Trim the fat from the kidneys, add them to the pan, and sear them on all sides until they lose their red color. Add the chicken bouillon, Burgundy wine, salt and pepper. Reduce the heat and simmer, covered, for 1½ hours. Remove the kidneys and slice them crosswise. Skim the fat from the sauce, and cook the sauce over high heat, uncovered, until the liquid is reduced to a scant cup.

Strain the sauce and discard the vegetables. Remove from the heat, and stir in the evaporated milk mixed with the Dijon mustard. Replace the kidneys in the pan and heat them in their sauce, but do not boil.

SERVES 6 · Approximately 220 to 250 calories each serving

Leeks with Chopped Egg

12 leeks
1 tablespoon butter
¾ cup chicken stock, or 1 chicken bouillon cube dissolved in ¾ cup water
1 teaspoon lemon juice
2 hard-cooked eggs, chopped fine

Trim the leeks, leaving about 1 inch of the green part. Cut the leeks almost up to but not through the root end. Hold them under running water and wash them well. Melt the butter in a heavy skillet and sauté the leeks for 2 minutes, turning them once. Add the stock and lemon juice and simmer the leeks, covered, for 30 minutes, or until they are tender. Place the leeks on a serving platter. Over high heat, reduce the pan juices to a few spoonfuls and pour over the leeks. Top with the chopped eggs.

SERVES 6 · Approximately 60 to 70 calories each serving

15

Crisp-Fried Mushrooms
Bite-Size Meatballs
Green Noodles (small portions)
Vanilla Butter Cake
Tea or Coffee with Approved Artificial Sweetener and Skim Milk

Crisp-Fried Mushrooms

1 pound mushrooms
1 tablespoon oil, approximately
Garlic powder
Salt
Coarse black pepper
3 tablespoons minced parsley

Slice the mushroom stems; quarter the caps. Heat a heavy skillet and add enough oil just to film the bottom. Sauté the mushrooms, stirring constantly, for 2 or 3 minutes. Sprinkle with garlic powder, salt, and black pepper to taste. As soon as the mushrooms appear the least bit moist, remove them from the heat. Add the parsley and serve immediately.

SERVES 6 · Approximately 30 to 40 calories each serving

Bite-Size Meatballs

1½ slices of whole-wheat bread, crusts removed
¾ pound lean beef
¾ pound veal
2 ounces ham, minced
2 eggs, lightly beaten
1 tablespoon A.1. Sauce
1 tablespoon minced scallion
1 teaspoon butter
1 tablespoon minced parsley
Salt
⅛ teaspoon grated nutmeg
⅛ teaspoon white pepper
2 tablespoons shortening
3 tablespoons flour
2¼ cups chicken stock
1 teaspoon prepared mustard
1 teaspoon soy sauce

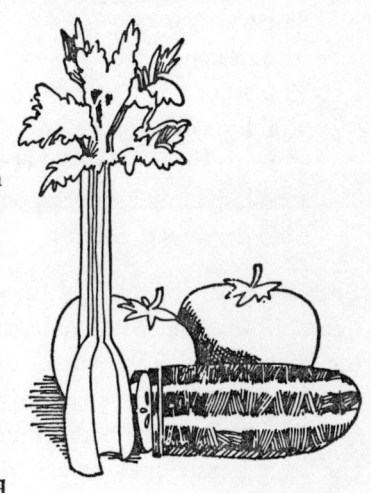

Soak the bread in water for 1 minute, and squeeze dry. Have the beef and veal ground together and work in the ham. Mix the bread with the eggs, 1 tablespoon water, A.1. Sauce, scallions which have been sautéed in the butter for 1 minute, the parsley, 1 teaspoon salt, the nutmeg and pepper. Add the meat, work the mixture well with your hands, and form it into about 3 dozen small meatballs.

Melt half of the shortening in a heavy skillet and brown the meatballs, a portion at a time, over high heat, shaking the pan to brown them evenly and keep them round. As you brown the meatballs, transfer them to a heavy saucepan. Scrape any burned particles from the skillet in which you browned the meatballs. In the same skillet, melt the remaining shortening and blend in the flour. Gradually add the chicken stock and cook the sauce, stirring constantly, until it is thick. Add the mustard and soy sauce. Pour the sauce over the meatballs and simmer them, covered, for 5 minutes.

SERVES 6 · Approximately 350 to 375 calories each serving

Vanilla Butter Cake

2 eggs
⅔ cup sugar
⅔ cup flour
⅔ teaspoon baking powder
3 tablespoons hot water
½ teaspoon vanilla extract
1 tablespoon plus 1 teaspoon melted butter, cooled
Fine dry bread crumbs

Beat the eggs lightly, add the sugar, and beat until thick and light. Sift the flour with the baking powder and stir half of it into the beaten eggs. Then stir in the water mixed with the vanilla, and finally stir in the remaining flour mixture. Fold in the butter quickly and pour the batter into a loaf pan (4 by 8 inches) that has been greased and dusted with bread crumbs. Bake in a preheated 350°F. oven for 40 minutes, or until the top of the cake springs back when pressed lightly. Turn out onto a rack and cool.

SERVES 6 · Approximately 175 to 195 calories each serving

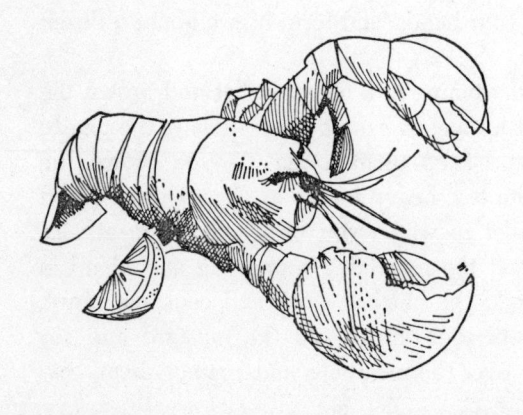

16

Crudités (An assortment of raw vegetables, such as cauliflowerets, carrot sticks, radishes, zucchini julienne, etc.)
* *Baked Lobster Stew*
New Potatoes Sprinkled with Minced Dill
* *Raspberry Cream Profiteroles*
Tea or Coffee with Approved Artificial Sweetener and Skim Milk

Baked Lobster Stew

3 lobsters, 1½ pounds each
1 tablespoon vegetable oil
6 medium-large tomatoes, peeled, seeded, and chopped
1 large onion, chopped
2 tablespoons minced parsley
1 teaspoon dried tarragon
½ teaspoon salt
1 garlic clove, crushed
1 cup clam juice
1 cup dry white wine
½ cup water
2 tablespoons butter
1 teaspoon lemon juice

Split the lobsters into halves; discard the sac behind the eyes and the intestinal vein. Reserve the tomalley and the coral, if there is any. Crack the claws of the lobsters and cut each half of the bodies into 4 or 5 pieces. Pour the oil into a Dutch oven or heavy pan and swirl the pan to coat the bottom lightly with oil. Add the lobsters, cover the pan, and cook over high heat until the shells turn bright red. Remove the lobster pieces from the pan. Add the tomatoes, onion, parsley, tarragon, salt and garlic to the pan, and stir until mixed. Arrange the lobsters on the vegetables and pour in the clam juice, wine and water. Cover and bake in a preheated 350°F. oven for 30 minutes. Transfer the lobster to a tureen or casserole that can come to the table. Mix the reserved tomalley and coral with the butter and lemon juice. Heat the stew almost to the boiling point. Remove from the heat and swirl in the butter mixture. Pour over the lobster and serve immediately.

SERVES 6 · Approximately 220 to 240 calories each serving

Raspberry Cream Profiteroles

2 tablespoons butter, cut into pieces
¼ cup boiling water
¼ cup flour
1 egg
⅔ cup whipped topping, or vanilla or strawberry ice milk
1 pint raspberries
1 tablespoon sugar

In a small saucepan over medium heat bring the butter and water to a boil. Add the flour and stir vigorously until the mixture comes away from the sides of the pan and forms a ball. Turn into the small bowl of an electric mixer and add the egg, beating thoroughly until the mixture is satiny. Drop 18 mounds, ¾ inch in diameter, on a greased cooky sheet. Space the mounds about 1 inch apart. Bake in a preheated 375°F. oven for 20 minutes. Cool the puffs.

Split the puffs horizontally into halves, and fill them with the whipped topping or vanilla or strawberry ice milk. Crush the raspberries with a fork and add the sugar. Place 3 filled profiteroles on each dessert plate. Spoon the raspberry sauce on top and serve immediately.

SERVES 6 · Approximately 120 to 130 calories each serving

17

Matzoth-Ball Soup
Norwegian Meat Patties in Cheese Sauce
Baked Tomatoes
Oatmeal Rounds
Marble Chiffon (Prepare 1 package each—4 servings each—of vanilla and chocolate chiffon-type pudding. Spoon into serving bowl, alternating vanilla and chocolate.)
Tea or Coffee with Approved Artificial Sweetener and Skim Milk

Matzoth-Ball Soup

2 eggs
⅓ cup very cold sparkling water
Pinch of ground ginger
½ teaspoon salt
2 tablespoons minced parsley
⅔ cup matzoth meal
6 cups well-seasoned chicken stock, or 8 chicken bouillon cubes dissolved in 6 cups water
1 large carrot, scraped and diced
2 celery ribs, sliced
¼ cup chopped onion

Beat the eggs, stir in the sparkling water, ginger, salt and parsley, and mix well. Stir in the matzoth meal and chill for several hours. Bring the stock to a boil and add the carrot, celery and onion. With wet hands, shape the matzoth-meal mixture into approximately 36 balls, about ¾ inch in diameter. Add them to the soup. Reduce the heat, cover the saucepan, and simmer for 35 minutes. Add water if necessary to maintain the amount of liquid.

SERVES 6 · Approximately 125 to 150 calories each serving

Norwegian Meat Patties in Cheese Sauce

- 1 egg, lightly beaten
- ⅓ cup water
- 2 tablespoons grated onion
- 2 tablespoons wheat germ
- 1 rounded tablespoon drained capers, mashed
- ½ teaspoon salt
- ⅛ teaspoon white pepper
- 1 pound lean beef
- ⅔ pound veal
- Vegetable shortening
- 1 tablespoon flour
- 2 cups chicken stock, or 2 chicken bouillon cubes dissolved in 2 cups water
- 1 tablespoon catsup
- 1 ounce Norwegian goat cheese (Gjetost), grated
- 1 teaspoon paprika

In a bowl mix the egg, water, onion, wheat germ, capers, salt and pepper. Add the beef and veal, and mix with your hands until well blended. Shape into 18 patties about ½ inch thick. Melt enough shortening in a large heavy iron skillet to coat the bottom of the pan lightly. Brown the patties on both sides over fairly high heat, adding more shortening as needed. Remove the patties as they are browned and set aside.

In a saucepan, mix the flour with a little of the chicken stock. Gradually add the remaining stock and cook over medium heat, stirring constantly, until the sauce thickens. Add the catsup, cheese and paprika, and stir until the cheese is melted.

Return the reserved patties to the skillet. Pour the sauce

over them and simmer for 10 to 15 minutes, adding more stock if the sauce thickens too much.

SERVES 6 · Approximately 260 to 280 calories each serving

Oatmeal Rounds

2 slices of firm-textured oatmeal bread
2 teaspoons butter

Trim the crusts from the bread and roll each slice with a rolling pin to flatten it a bit. Spread the butter on the bread, roll each piece tightly, and cut each roll into 3 equal pieces. Secure with food picks. Bake in a preheated 400°F. oven for 15 to 20 minutes, or until they take on some color. Remove picks and serve.

MAKES 6 rounds · Approximately 22 calories each round

18

Shrimps Marinara
Polish Knedle
Boston Lettuce Salad
Lemon Snowballs (Scoop out balls of lemon sherbet
and roll them in shredded or flaked coconut.)
*Tea or Coffee with Approved Artificial Sweetener
and Skim Milk*

~~~

Shrimps Marinara

½ tablespoon vegetable oil
½ tablespoon butter
1 medium-size onion, chopped fine
1 large can (32 ounces) Italian plum tomatoes

1 tablespoon sugar
2 teaspoons dried basil
1 teaspoon salt
¼ teaspoon coarse black pepper
4 to 4½ dozen large shrimps, cooked and cleaned

Place the oil and butter in an enamelware saucepan, heat until foaming, and add the onion. Reduce the heat and cook, stirring frequently, until the onion is translucent. Add the tomatoes and crush the pulp. Add the sugar, basil, salt and pepper and simmer, uncovered, until the juices have evaporated, about 1 hour. Add the shrimps and cook until just heated through. Do not overcook. Serve immediately.

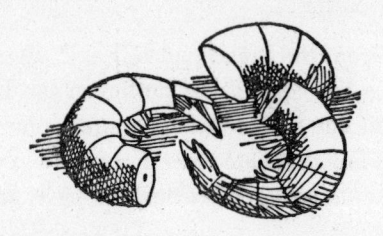

SERVES 6 · Approximately 250 to 280 calories each serving

Note: To make a richer marinara sauce, increase the oil and butter each to 2 to 3 tablespoons.

Polish Knedle

¾ cup sieved cottage cheese
1 tablespoon softened butter
⅓ cup farina
¼ cup freshly grated Parmesan cheese
3 eggs, separated
Salt and pepper

Beat the cottage cheese, butter, farina, Parmesan cheese and egg yolks until the mixture is smooth. Add salt and pepper to taste. Beat the egg whites until stiff but not dry, and fold them into the batter. Butter 6 muffin cups and spoon the batter into them.

Set them into a large pan containing ½ inch of simmering water. Cover the pan and steam the molds over medium heat for 30 minutes. Remove the *knedle* from the custard cups and serve immediately.

SERVES 6 · Approximately 140 to 160 calories each serving

Note: To make dessert *knedle*, eliminate the Parmesan cheese, add a little sugar to taste to the batter, and serve with a little honey, sugar and cinnamon, or low-calorie jam.

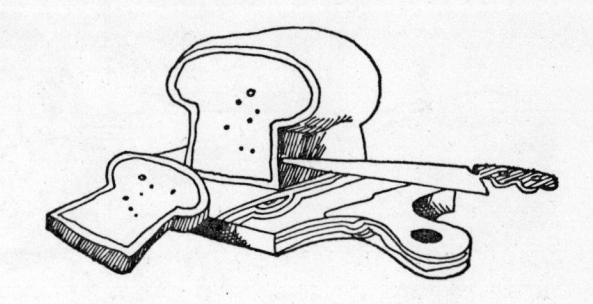

SWEET

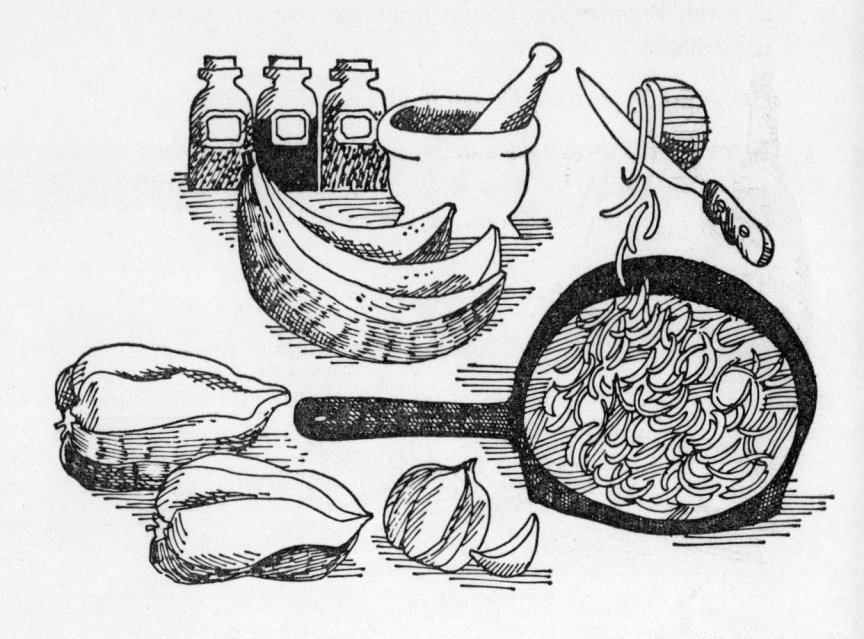

1. Mixed Green Salad with Low-calorie Dressing
   * Breast of Chicken Country Captain 171
   Steamed Low-calorie Rice
   * Apple and Banana Fluff 172

2. Frosty Tomato Juice
   Grilled Lamb Chop
   * Cheese-Creamed Spinach 173
   * Sweet Pepper Ragout 174
   * Flaming Pineapple and Strawberries Glacé 174

3. Melon
   * Trout Baked in Caper Sauce 175
   Steamed Broccoli
   * Spicy Apple Cake 176

4. Cranberry Freeze
   * Sweet-Stuffed Veal Chop 177
   Steamed Parsleyed Cauliflower
   * Orange Pineapple Ring 178

   (* indicates recipe is given)

DINNERS

5 * Beef Orientale 179
　　Steamed Low-calorie Rice
　　Bean Sprouts
　* Red Fruits 180

6 * Delicate Curry of Lamb 181
　* Curry Accompaniments 182
　　Cucumber Chunks
　* Spring Mold 182

7 * Mushroom Bisque 183
　* Calves' Brains Piquant 184
　　Orange Carrots
　* Pineapple Cheese 185

8　Bowl of Cherry Tomatoes and Egg Tomatoes
　* Sweet and Sour Fish 186
　　Party Rye Toast
　* Individual Soufflés Bacchus 187

9　Bibb Lettuce Mimosa
　* Summer Chicken and Melon Sagaro 188
　　Sesame Crackers
　* Filled Gossamer Crêpes 189

　　(* indicates recipe is given)

10   Broiled Grapefruit
    * Veal Kidneys Duc d'Anjou   190
      Tiny Frozen Peas
    * Stained Glass Window Dessert   191

11   Beefsteak Tomatoes
    * Pot Roast with Sauerkraut   192
      Baked Potato
    * Fizzy Fruits   193

12   Fringed Celery
      Roast Leg of Lamb with Mint Jelly
    * Eggplant Normande   194
    * Chocolate Fruit Fondu   194

13   Asparagus Vinaigrette
    * Viennese Chicken Livers, Onions and Apples   195
      Low-calorie Rice
    * Peppermint Pineapple   196

14   Cantaloupe Rings Laced with Port
    * Spicy Shell Steaks   197
      French Bread
      Watercress
    * Marinated Peaches   198

15   Melon Balls in Melon
    * Ed Giobbi's Chicken with Mussels   198
      Italian Bread
      Escarole
    * Strawberries Diane   199

16 * Blender Soup Argenteuil   200
    * Cold Poached Halibut with Tiny Shrimps   201
      Sweet Cucumber Slices
    * Apple Soufflés à la Russe   202

17 * Ripe Tomato Soup   203
    * Sweetbreads Baumanière   203
    * Parsleyed Peas and Cucumbers   204
      Strawberries in Strawberry Glaze

18 * Hububub   205
    * Chicken in Cider Sauce   205
    * Lin's Water Chestnuts and Celery   206
      Fruits Rafraîchis

1

Mixed Green Salad with any Low-calorie Diet Dressing
* Breast of Chicken Country Captain
Steamed Low-calorie Rice (available in health food stores)
* Apple and Banana Fluff
*Tea or Coffee with Approved Artificial Sweetener
and Skim Milk*

Breast of Chicken Country Captain

6 breasts of chicken (3 whole breasts cut into halves), wings removed
1 large green pepper, seeded and cut into strips ½ inch wide
½ small sweet red pepper, seeded and cut into strips ½ inch wide
1 large onion, diced
1¼ teaspoons curry powder
1 large tomato, peeled, seeded, and chopped into coarse pieces
1 can (1 pound) plum tomatoes
1½ teaspoons ground mace
¾ teaspoon salt
⅛ teaspoon coarse black pepper
1½ tablespoons fresh tarragon, or 1½ teaspoons dried tarragon
1 garlic clove, mashed
3 tablespoons raisins
2 tablespoons orange marmalade

Brown the pieces of chicken in a heavy skillet over medium heat; there should be enough fat in the chicken itself to brown it in. As the pieces are browned, arrange them in a single layer in a shallow baking dish that can come to the table.

In the same skillet, over low heat, sauté the peppers and onion for 15 minutes, stirring frequently. Add the curry powder and sauté for 3 minutes. Add the remaining ingredients and simmer, stirring occasionally, for 20 to 30 minutes, or until the sauce is quite thick. Adjust seasonings. Spoon the sauce over the chicken and bake, covered, in a preheated 350°F. oven for about 40 minutes, or until tender.

SERVES 6 · Approximately 275 to 300 calories each serving

Apple and Banana Fluff

1½ envelopes unflavored gelatin
¼ cup cold water
3 eggs
¼ cup sugar
3 medium-size very ripe bananas
Thick applesauce, canned or homemade, with as little sugar as possible (about ⅔ cup)
1 teaspoon almond extract
2 tablespoons sour cream
Freshly grated nutmeg

Soak the gelatin in the cold water in a small saucepan, dissolve over low heat, and cool. Beat the eggs and sugar in an electric mixer at high speed for 10 minutes, or until thick and light. Meanwhile, mash the bananas and add enough applesauce to make a generous 2 cups altogether. Stir in the almond extract, sour cream and gelatin. Fold in the egg-sugar mixture. Pour into 6 dessert dishes and sprinkle with nutmeg. Chill until set.

SERVES 6 · Approximately 165 to 200 calories each serving

2

Frosty Tomato Juice
Grilled Lamb Chop
* Cheese-Creamed Spinach
* Sweet Pepper Ragout
* Flaming Pineapple and Strawberries Glacé
*Tea or Coffee with Approved Artificial Sweetener
and Skim Milk*

Cheese-Creamed Spinach

3 packages (10 ounces each) frozen chopped spinach
½ cup creamed small-curd cottage cheese
1 tablespoon heavy cream
Pinch of ground mace
Salt and pepper

Cook the spinach according to package directions and drain, but do not press out any of the liquid. Reserve a few spoonfuls of the drained liquid. Mix the cottage cheese, cream and mace with the spinach and purée, half at a time, in an electric blender. It may be necessary to turn the motor off and scrape down the sides with a rubber spatula if the ingredients are not being properly puréed. It may also be necessary to add a spoonful of the reserved liquid. Season with salt and pepper to taste.

SERVES 6 · Approximately 45 to 55 calories each serving

Sweet Pepper Ragout

- 2 medium-size onions, minced
- 2 garlic cloves, mashed
- 1 tablespoon olive oil
- 1 tablespoon flour
- 2 beef bouillon cubes
- 1½ cups hot water
- 4 teaspoons catsup
- 1 teaspoon paprika
- 3 large sweet red peppers, seeded and cut into strips 1 inch wide
- 3 large green peppers, seeded and cut into strips 1 inch wide
- Salt and pepper

In a large heavy saucepan, over medium heat, sauté the onions and the garlic in the oil until the onions are golden brown. Sprinkle with flour and cook, stirring constantly, for 1 minute. Dissolve the bouillon cubes in the water, gradually add to the onion mixture, and cook until thickened, stirring occasionally. Add the catsup, paprika and red and green peppers. Cover the saucepan and simmer over low heat for 30 minutes, or until the peppers are tender. Add salt and pepper to taste.

SERVES 6 · Approximately 50 to 60 calories each serving

Flaming Pineapple and Strawberries Glacé

- 1 can (8 ounces) unsweetened pineapple tidbits
- 2 teaspoons butter
- 3 tablespoons sugar
- 1 pint ripe strawberries
- 1 pint vanilla or strawberry ice milk, divided into 6 scoops
- 3 tablespoons Cognac

Drain the pineapple, reserving the juice in a small pitcher. Melt the butter in the blazer of a chafing dish over direct heat. Add the sugar and cook for 1 minute. Add the pineapple and the strawberries and cook, stirring constantly, until the berries are thoroughly heated. Place a scoop of ice milk in each of 6 dessert dishes. Add the Cognac to the fruit, heat for a few seconds, and ignite. When the flames die out, pour in the reserved pineapple juice. Ladle fruit and juices over the ice milk and serve immediately.

Note: If you do not have a chafing dish, use an electric skillet or a saucepan attractive enough to be brought to the table. After the Cognac has been heated, bring the fruit to the table, ignite the Cognac, add the pineapple juice, and proceed as above.

SERVES 6 · Approximately 140 to 160 calories each serving

3

Slice of Crenshaw, Cantaloupe, or Honeydew Melon
* Trout Baked in Caper Sauce
Steamed Broccoli
* Spicy Apple Cake
*Tea or Coffee with Approved Artificial Sweetener
and Skim Milk*

Trout Baked in Caper Sauce

6 brook trout, about ⅔ pound each
1½ teaspoons seasoned salt
½ teaspoon seasoned pepper
½ cup dry white wine
2 tablespoons dry vermouth
1 chicken bouillon cube dissolved in 2 tablespoons hot water
1 tablespoon butter
2½ tablespoons flour
⅔ cup milk
2 tablespoons capers, mashed

Sprinkle the insides of the fish with the seasoned salt and seasoned pepper. Place them in a large skillet and pour the combined wine, vermouth, and dissolved bouillon cube over the fish. Cover and simmer over low heat for 15 minutes, or until the fish flakes easily. Cool the fish in the stock for 10 minutes, or until you can handle them. Remove the skin and bones. (The sooner you do this, the easier it is to remove the skin.) Place the fillets side by side in a lightly greased shallow baking dish, preferably one that can come to the table. Strain the stock and add water, if necessary, to make 1½ cups liquid.

Melt the butter in a saucepan. Blend in the flour and cook for 1 minute, stirring constantly. Gradually add the milk and the reserved stock. Cook over low heat, stirring constantly, until the sauce has thickened. Add the capers and spoon over the fish. (Preparation up to this point may be done in advance.)

About 30 minutes before serving time, place the fish in a preheated 375°F. oven for 20 to 25 minutes, or until the sauce is bubbling.

SERVES 6 · Approximately 325 to 375 calories each serving

Spicy Apple Cake

2 tablespoons butter
¼ cup light brown sugar
¼ cup dark brown sugar
½ beaten egg
½ cup flour
¼ teaspoon baking powder
⅛ teaspoon baking soda
½ teaspoon ground cinnamon
¼ teaspoon ground ginger
2 small apples, peeled, cored, and sliced

Cream the butter and sugars. Beat in the egg. (To measure ½ egg, beat the egg lightly first, then measure. A whole egg, government graded "large," generally measures about ¼ cup.) Sift together all the dry ingredients and stir into the creamed mixture. Fold in the apples so that they are coated with batter. Spoon into a greased pie plate (8 or 9 inches) and bake in a preheated 350°F. oven for 30 to 35 minutes, or until the cake starts to shrink from the plate. Serve warm or at room temperature, plain or with whipped low-calorie topping or a small scoop of ice milk.

SERVES 6 · Approximately 145 to 155 calories each serving, without ice milk or topping

4

Cranberry Freeze (low-calorie cranberry-juice cocktail over crushed ice)
* Sweet-Stuffed Veal Chop
Steamed Parsleyed Cauliflower
* Orange Pineapple Ring
Tea or Coffee with Approved Artificial Sweetener and Skim Milk

Sweet-Stuffed Veal Chop

6 loin veal chops, each ¾ inch thick
1 tablespoon butter
⅓ cup minced ham
3 tablespoons seeded raisins
2 tablespoons pine nuts
1 tablespoon minced parsley
2 tablespoons Escoffier Sauce Robert
Salt
2 tablespoons dry sherry
1 cup chicken stock
Flour
Sour cream

Have the butcher cut a pocket in each of the chops. Melt half of the butter in a heavy skillet, add the ham, and cook for 1 minute. Remove the skillet from the heat and add the raisins, nuts, parsley, 1 tablespoon of the Sauce Robert, and salt to taste. Coat the interior of the veal chop pockets with the remaining Sauce Robert, and fill the pockets with the ham mixture. Secure the openings with small skewers or food picks. Melt the remaining butter in the skillet, and brown the chops in it. Remove the chops to another pan and pour the sherry over them. Deglaze the skillet with the chicken stock and pour the pan juices over the chops. Simmer them, covered, over low heat for 30 minutes, or until tender.

Remove the chops to a platter, remove the skewers, and keep the chops warm. Strain the pan juices and measure them. For each cup of liquid, mix 1 tablespoon each of flour and sour cream. Combine this with the pan juices and boil the sauce over medium heat, stirring constantly until thickened. Pour the sauce over the chops and serve immediately.

SERVES 6 · Approximately 350 to 375 calories each serving

Orange Pineapple Ring

- 1 can (14 ounces) sliced unsweetened pineapple
- 1 envelope (4 servings) low-calorie orange-flavored gelatin dessert
- ¼ cup orange juice
- ½ large banana, sliced thin

Drain the pineapple, measure the juice, and add water to make 1 cup. Heat the liquid, add the gelatin, and stir until dissolved. Add the orange juice. Rinse a 4-cup ring mold with cold water and pour in a thin layer of gelatin. Place in a freezer for a few minutes, until almost set. Place the banana slices, slightly overlapping, on top of the gelatin. Chop the pineapple fine, add to the liquid gelatin, and pour into the mold. Chill for several hours, or until set. With the tip of a small sharp knife, loosen the gelatin from the mold, dip the mold into hot water for a few seconds, and invert onto a serving platter.

SERVES 6 · Approximately 45 to 55 calories each serving

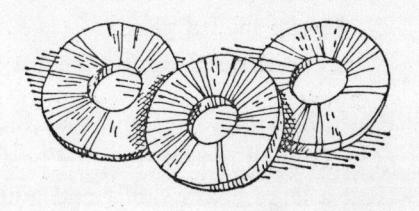

5

Beef Orientale
Steamed Low-calorie Rice (available in health-food stores)
Bean Sprouts (Heat canned bean sprouts and dress with soy sauce.)
* Red Fruits
Tea or Coffee with Approved Artificial Sweetener and Skim Milk

Beef Orientale

3 dried Chinese mushrooms
2½ pounds beef bottom round
1 tablespoon peanut oil
1 large onion, minced
1 large garlic clove, mashed
1 tablespoon soy sauce
2 tablespoons dark brown sugar
1½ cups beef consommé
3 tablespoons tomato paste
Salt

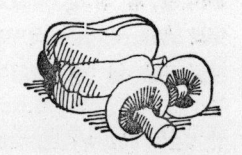

¾ teaspoon ground ginger
1 teaspoon granulated sugar
⅓ cup flour
1¼ cups water
¾ cup shelled peas
1 cup slivered bamboo shoots

Wash the mushrooms and soak them in cold water for 30 minutes. Trim all the fat from the beef and cut it into 1-inch cubes. Heat a large heavy skillet and add the oil. Over high heat sear the meat, a portion at a time, and transfer it to a heatproof casserole. Add the onion, cover the casserole, and bake in a preheated 300°F. oven for 30 minutes. Drain the mushrooms, cut them into thin strips, and add them to the meat with the garlic, soy sauce, brown sugar, beef consommé, tomato paste, ¾ teaspoon salt, the ginger and granulated sugar. Bake, covered, for 1¼ hours, or until the meat is tender. Skim off the fat. Mix the flour and water, add to the meat, and cook over direct heat, stirring constantly, until the sauce thickens. Taste, and add salt if necessary. Add the peas and bamboo shoots and cook over medium heat until the peas are tender but still crisp.

SERVES 6 · Approximately 400 to 450 calories each serving

Red Fruits

2 tablespoons framboise or kirsch
3 cups very sweet ripe watermelon balls
¾ cup very ripe raspberries
18 pitted large Bing cherries

Spoon the liqueur over the melon balls and chill for 1 hour or longer, stirring occasionally. Divide the melon balls among 6 dessert dishes, reserving all the juice. Arrange the raspberries and cherries on top and dribble the reserved juice over all.

SERVES 6 · Approximately 60 to 70 calories each serving

6

Delicate Curry of Lamb
Curry Accompaniments
Cucumber Chunks (peeled, seeded, and diced cucumber,
mixed with salt and yoghurt to taste)
Spring Mold
Tea or Coffee with Approved Artificial Sweetener
and Skim Milk

~~~~

Delicate Curry of Lamb

2 leeks, trimmed and sliced thin
2 celery ribs, minced
1 tablespoon butter
2½ pounds boneless lean lamb, cut into 2-inch cubes
2 tablespoons flour
2 teaspoons mild curry powder
¼ teaspoon white pepper
¼ teaspoon ground cinnamon
Salt
1½ tablespoons minced preserved gingerroot
5 tablespoons low-calorie pineapple jam
2 teaspoons lime juice
1 garlic clove, mashed
¼ cup light raisins
1 cup beef stock
1 cup plus 2 tablespoons milk
2 cups honeydew melon balls or ¾-inch melon cubes

In a Dutch oven, over low heat, sauté the leeks and celery in the butter until tender but not brown. Raise the heat to medium, add the lamb, and sear the pieces of meat on all sides. Mix 1 tablespoon of the flour with the curry powder, pepper, cinnamon, and 2 teaspoons of salt. Add to the meat, stirring constantly. Now add the preserved gingerroot, the low-calorie pineapple jam, the lime juice, garlic, raisins, beef stock, and 1 cup of the milk. Bring to the boil, reduce the heat and simmer, covered, for 1 hour, or until the meat is tender. Add the melon, uncover, and cook over high heat for 5 minutes. Skim the fat; taste and add salt if necessary. Mix the remaining flour with the remaining milk. Stir in a little of the hot curry sauce, then return the whole to the pot and cook, stirring constantly, until thickened.

SERVES 6 · Approximately 325 to 375 calories each serving

Curry Accompaniments

Surround the curry with these accompaniments, each in a small dish, so that they may be passed around for people to serve themselves.

- 2 hard-cooked egg yolks, crumbled
- 2 hard-cooked egg whites, riced or minced
- 1½ cups Wheat or Rice Chex, toasted in the oven and crumbled
- 3 leeks, including a little of the green part, trimmed and sliced thin
- 1 small banana, sliced just before serving time

Spring Mold

- 1 envelope unflavored gelatin
- 2 tablespoons cold water
- ½ pound tender young rhubarb, diced
- ½ cup sugar
- 2 tablespoons red Dubonnet
- 1½ cups ripe strawberries
- 2 tablespoons low-calorie strawberry jam
- ¼ cup heavy cream, whipped until stiff
- 1 egg white

Soften the gelatin in the cold water. Bring the rhubarb and 6 tablespoons of the sugar to a boil, stirring constantly to prevent burning. Lower the heat and simmer the rhubarb until it falls apart. Dissolve the softened gelatin in the hot rhubarb, remove from the heat, and add the Dubonnet and half of the strawberries that have been mashed with the low-calorie strawberry jam. Chill the mixture until it starts to set. Fold in the cream and the egg white that has been whipped until stiff with the remaining sugar. Pour into a mold that has been rinsed in cold water. Chill until set, turn out onto a serving platter, and garnish with the remaining strawberries.

SERVES 6 · Approximately 130 to 145 calories each serving

7

Mushroom Bisque
Calves' Brains Piquant
Orange Carrots (sliced and steamed carrots with a sprinkling of grated orange rind)
Pineapple Cheese
Tea or Coffee with Approved Artificial Sweetener and Skim Milk

Mushroom Bisque

1 pound fresh mushrooms, sliced ¼ inch thick
1 teaspoon butter
1 teaspoon lemon juice
1 cup water
¾ teaspoon salt
1 teaspoon dried tarragon
½ teaspoon dried chervil
Pinch of white pepper

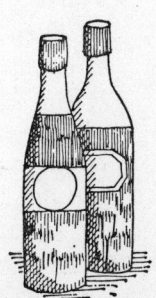

1½ cups beef bouillon, or 2 beef bouillon cubes dissolved in 1½ cups water
3 tablespoons flour
2 tablespoons sour cream
1 cup skim milk
2 tablespoons Madeira

Place the mushrooms in a saucepan with the butter, lemon juice, 1 cup water, salt, tarragon, chervil and pepper. Bring to a boil, reduce the heat and simmer, covered, for 5 minutes. Add the bouillon and simmer for another minute or two.

In a small bowl, mix the flour and sour cream. Gradually add the milk and stir with a whisk until smooth. Pour in a few spoonfuls of the hot bouillon, then return the mixture to the saucepan. Cook, stirring constantly, until the bisque thickens. Stir in the Madeira. Taste and add more seasoning if necessary. Serve immediately or reheat carefully at serving time.

SERVES 6 · Approximately 65 to 75 calories each serving

Calves' Brains Piquant

3 pairs calves' brains
Salt
6 peppercorns
3 cloves
3 tablespoons lemon juice
1 carrot, scraped and sliced
1 onion, chopped into coarse pieces
3 tablespoons butter
⅓ cup flour
⅓ cup Curaçao
3 tablespoons drained capers
Dash of white pepper
1½ tablespoons fine bread crumbs

Soak the brains in cold water for 1 hour. Plunge into boiling water for 1 minute, drain, and peel off as much as possible of the covering membrane.

In a large saucepan, place 1½ quarts water, 1 teaspoon salt, the peppercorns, cloves, 2 tablespoons of the lemon juice, the carrot and onion. Bring to the boil, reduce the heat, add the brains, and simmer over low heat for 20 minutes. Remove the brains, cut into bite-sized pieces, and arrange in a shallow ovenproof dish that can come to the table. Strain the stock and reserve.

In another saucepan, melt the butter. Blend in the flour, then gradually add 1 quart of the reserved stock and the remaining lemon juice. Raise the heat and boil, stirring occasionally, until the sauce is thickened and reduced to about half. Add the Curaçao and the capers and cook for 1 minute longer. Add salt to taste and the pepper. Pour the sauce over the brains and sprinkle the bread crumbs on top. Bake in a preheated 450°F. for 10 minutes and serve.

SERVES 6 · Approximately 325 to 350 calories each serving

Pineapple Cheese

1 can (14 ounces) unsweetened sliced pineapple
1 envelope unflavored gelatin
1 egg, separated
½ cup light brown sugar
1 tablespoon grated lemon rind
1 tablespoon lemon juice
½ pound cottage cheese, sieved
¼ cup heavy cream, whipped until stiff

Drain the pineapple thoroughly and measure the juice. Add water if necessary to measure 1 cup liquid. Chop the pineapple and reserve. Soften the gelatin in the liquid. In a saucepan, combine the egg yolk, brown sugar, lemon rind and juice. Add the gelatin mixture and cook over low heat, stirring constantly, until the sugar is dissolved. Add the cottage cheese and chill until the mixture starts to set. Fold in the reserved pineapple, the whipped cream, and the egg white that has been whipped until stiff. Pour into a decorative bowl that can come to the table. Chill for several hours, and serve in the bowl.

SERVES 6 · Approximately 170 to 190 calories each serving

8

*Bowl of Chilled Cherry Tomatoes and Egg Tomatoes
(presented with a shaker of seasoned salt)
* Sweet and Sour Fish
Party Rye Toast (small squares of party rye bread,
toasted and served hot)
* Individual Soufflés Bacchus
Tea or Coffee with Approved Artificial Sweetener
and Skim Milk*

Sweet and Sour Fish

3 pounds flounder fillets
2 cups water
6 peppercorns
2 bay leaves
4 tablespoons vinegar
½ teaspoon salt
8 small gingersnaps
¼ cup dark brown sugar
¼ cup light raisins
6 thin lemon slices

Have the fillets cut lengthwise into halves. Fold each piece in half, or roll and secure with a food pick. In a large skillet or saucepan, combine 2 cups water, the peppercorns, bay leaves, half of the vinegar, and the salt. Bring to a boil. Add the fish in a single layer and simmer, covered, over low heat for 12 to 15 minutes, or until the fish flakes easily. Lift out the fish and place on a serving dish. Keep it hot if you plan to serve it hot. Reserve the stock, strain it, measure and add water, if necessary, to make 1½ cups. Pour into a saucepan and add the gingersnaps, remaining vinegar, the brown sugar and raisins. Cook, stirring constantly, until thickened and smooth. Add more salt if necessary. Pour over the fish. Garnish with lemon slices. Serve immediately if it is to be eaten hot. Otherwise, cool and chill.

SERVES 6 · Approximately 200 to 225 calories each serving

Individual Soufflés Bacchus

¾ pound red or black grapes, seeded and cut into quarters, or ¾ pound seedless grapes, cut into halves
⅓ cup any preferred low-calorie jam
⅓ cup sugar
⅓ cup flour
⅛ teaspoon salt
1¼ cups skim milk
5 eggs, separated
Confectioners' sugar

Mix the grapes with the jam and divide among 6 individual soufflé dishes or casseroles.

Preheat the oven to 400°F. In a saucepan, mix the sugar, flour and salt. Gradually add the skim milk and stir until smooth. Cook over medium heat, stirring constantly, until thick. Remove from the heat and add the egg yolks, lightly beaten. Beat the egg whites until stiff but not dry, fold into the batter, and spoon the soufflé mixture over the grapes. Place the soufflés in the oven, reduce the heat to 375°F., and bake for 15 minutes, or until the soufflés are puffed and golden. Dust generously with confectioners' sugar and serve.

SERVES 6 · Approximately 180 to 195 calories each serving

9

Bibb Lettuce Mimosa (Allow 1 large head per person, use any low-calorie dressing, and sprinkle crumbled egg yolk over lettuce at serving time.)
* *Summer Chicken and Melon Sagaro*
Sesame Crackers (crisped in the oven at serving time)
* *Filled Gossamer Crêpes*
Tea or Coffee with Approved Artificial Sweetener and Skim Milk

Summer Chicken and Melon Sagaro

- 2 cups well-seasoned chicken stock
- 2 celery ribs, sliced
- 2 carrots, scraped and sliced
- 4 whole breasts (8 halves) of 3½-pound fryers, without wings
- 1 large Spanish melon, or 1 large honeydew melon, or 3 cantaloupes
- Black pepper
- 1 lime

Bring the stock to a boil. Add the celery and carrots and cook for 5 minutes. Add the 8 halves of chicken breast and poach, covered, over low heat for about 25 minutes, or until tender. Cool the chicken in the stock, remove the skin and bones, and chill.

Cut the melon into 6 wedges and discard the seeds. Make as many melon balls as possible, then scoop out all the scraps with a spoon. Chill the melon and reserve the shells. Shortly before serving time divide the scraps of melon among the 6 shells. Cut the chicken into bite-size pieces, mix with the melon balls, and spoon into the shells. Sprinkle one or two grindings of coarse black pepper over each serving and garnish with a wedge of lime to squeeze over the melon and chicken.

SERVES 6 · Approximately 325 to 375 calories each serving

Filled Gossamer Crêpes

Double recipe of crêpe batter (see below)
¼ cup low-calorie jam
Confectioners' sugar

In advance, or an hour or so ahead of time, make 12 crêpes according to the basic crêpe recipe. Spread each crêpe with 1 teaspoon of jam, roll up, and place them side by side in a buttered shallow baking dish that can accommodate the rolled crêpes in a single layer. Refrigerate until shortly before serving time.

Cover the baking dish with foil and place in a preheated 450°F. oven for a few minutes until the crêpes are piping hot. Place 2 crêpes on each dessert plate and dust generously with confectioners' sugar.

SERVES 6 · Approximately 110 to 120 calories each serving

Basic Crêpes

1 egg
¼ cup flour
¼ cup milk
¼ cup sparkling water or plain water
About 1 teaspoon butter for frying

Beat the egg, add the flour, and beat again. Gradually pour in the milk and water and continue beating until the batter is smooth. It is best, though not essential, to prepare the batter an hour or so before frying the crêpes, to allow the flour to absorb all the liquid it can. If you do so, you may notice that the batter seems thicker after standing. Then, add a spoonful of milk if necessary to thin the batter slightly.

Heat a heavy 6- to 7-inch skillet over high heat until a speck of butter sizzles when dropped in. Brush the bottom of the pan with just enough butter to coat it. Ladle about 2 tablespoons of batter (about one cooking spoon) into the pan, tilting it so that the batter covers the bottom. Fry until slightly brown on the bottom and dry on top. Turn with a spatula or your fingers, fry the other side for 20 to 30 seconds, and tip out onto a board. Repeat until the batter is used up.

MAKES about 6 crêpes · Each crêpe has approximately 35 to 40 calories

10

Broiled Grapefruit (Spread a little honey on the surface before broiling.)
*Veal Kidneys Duc d'Anjou
Tiny Frozen Peas
*Stained Glass Window Dessert
Tea or Coffee with Approved Artificial Sweetener and Skim Milk

Veal Kidneys Duc d'Anjou

2 veal knuckles, cracked
2 celery ribs, cut into 1-inch pieces
1 large carrot, scraped and cut into 6 pieces
1 large onion, peeled and chopped
1 large bay leaf
½ teaspoon salt
5 peppercorns
6 veal kidneys, removed from their fat
3 tablespoons Cognac
6 tablespoons Curaçao
2 tablespoons butter

¼ cup flour
1½ teaspoons Dijon mustard
2 tablespoons minced parsley
2 tablespoons lemon juice
Salt and pepper

In a large pot, place the veal knuckles, celery, carrot, onion, bay leaf, salt and peppercorns. Cover with cold water, bring to a boil, cover, and simmer for 2 hours. Strain the stock and place it in the freezer until the fat rises to the surface. Skim off the fat, measure the stock, and add water if necessary to make 3 cups of liquid altogether.

Cut the kidneys lengthwise into halves; remove the inner cores and as much of the interior fat as possible. Cut the kidneys crosswise into ¼-inch-thick slices. In a large heavy skillet heat the Cognac and ignite it. Place the kidney slices in the pan, add half of the Curaçao, and continue to flame, basting the kidneys with the pan juices until the flames die out. Cook for 3 minutes longer, stirring constantly.

Melt the butter in a heavy saucepan over medium heat. Blend in the flour, then gradually add the reserved veal stock and cook, stirring constantly, until the sauce starts to thicken. Add the mustard, parsley and lemon juice. Cook over high heat until the sauce reduces to half. Add the kidneys and their juices to the sauce, then stir in the remaining Curaçao. Add salt and pepper to taste. Simmer just until the kidneys are heated through. Serve at once.

SERVES 6 · Approximately 260 to 295 calories each serving

Stained Glass Window Dessert

1 envelope (4 servings) low-calorie orange-flavored gelatin dessert
3⅔ cups hot water
1 envelope (4 servings) low-calorie lemon-flavored gelatin dessert
1 envelope (4 servings) low-calorie lime-flavored gelatin dessert
3 cups Cool Whip or other low-calorie whipped topping

Dissolve the orange gelatin in 1⅓ cups hot water, pour into an 8-inch square baking pan that has been rinsed in cold water, and chill until firm. Repeat with the lemon gelatin and an additional 1⅓ cups water. Dissolve the lime gelatin in the remaining 1 cup water, and chill until slightly thickened. Fold into the Cool Whip. When the orange and lemon gelatin are stiff, cut them into ½-inch cubes and fold into the cream mixture. Gently pack into a loaf pan (4 by 8 inches) that has been rinsed in cold water. Chill until firm. Unmold onto a platter and refrigerate until serving time.

SERVES 6 · Approximately 145 to 155 calories each serving

11

Beefsteak Tomatoes (chilled, peeled, and cut into thick slices, sprinkled with salt and dark brown sugar)
* *Pot Roast with Sauerkraut*
Small Baked Potato (or half of a large one)
* *Fizzy Fruits*
Tea or Coffee with Approved Artificial Sweetener and Skim Milk

Pot Roast with Sauerkraut

- 1 teaspoon salt
- 1 garlic clove, mashed
- ⅛ teaspoon coarse black pepper
- 2½ pounds beef bottom round
- 1 onion, sliced
- 2 cups water
- 1½ pounds sauerkraut, rinsed and drained
- ¼ cup tomato paste
- ¼ cup brown sugar
- ⅛ teaspoon ground cloves

Combine the salt, garlic and black pepper and rub them into the beef. Place the beef in a heavy roasting pan with the onion and ½ cup of the water. Roast, covered, in a preheated 400°F. oven for 1¼ hours, basting frequently. Place the sauerkraut around the meat. Stir together the tomato paste, remaining water, brown sugar and cloves, and pour over the sauerkraut. Reduce the heat to 350°F., cover the pan, and roast for 1½ hours longer, or until the meat is just tender. Baste frequently with the pan juices. Pour off the pan juices into a shallow pan and place the pan in a freezer so that the fat will rise to the surface and start to solidify. Skim off the fat. Arrange the sauerkraut around the edge, or in the middle of, a shallow ovenproof dish, preferably one that can come to the table. Cut the meat into ⅓-inch-thick slices and arrange the slices in the center of the ring of sauerkraut, or over the bed of sauerkraut. Pour the pan juices over the meat and cover. About 30 minutes before serving, reheat the meat in a 350°F. oven.

SERVES 6 · Approximately 375 to 425 calories each serving

Fizzy Fruits

1 cup carbonated lemon-flavored beverage (regular or low-calorie)
2 cups strawberries
1 cup blueberries
2 cups diced ripe pineapple
Lemon juice
2 tablespoons sugar

Chill the beverage thoroughly in the refrigerator or place the bottle in the freezer while preparing the fruit. Combine the strawberries, blueberries and pineapple in a shallow bowl that can come to the table. Squeeze a little lemon juice over the fruits, sprinkle with the sugar, toss lightly, and chill for an hour or longer. At serving time, pour 1 cup of the lemon drink over the fruit and serve immediately.

SERVES 6 · Approximately 75 to 90 calories each serving

12

Fringed Celery (3-inch lengths of celery, fringed at both ends and crisped in ice water. Serve with seasoned salt.)
Roast Leg of Lamb with Mint Jelly (3 medium-size slices of meat and 1 teaspoon jelly for each serving)
* *Eggplant Normande*
* *Chocolate Fruit Fondu*
Tea or Coffee with Approved Artificial Sweetener and Skim Milk

Eggplant Normande

2 pounds eggplant, about 2 medium-size
2 medium-size onions, minced
1 tablespoon butter
1 cup applesauce, canned or homemade
½ teaspoon dried marjoram
Salt

Peel the eggplant and boil in salted water to cover until tender. Drain well, pressing out as much liquid as possible. Sauté the onions in butter until tender and golden. Mash the eggplant, or purée in an electric blender with the sautéed onions, the applesauce and marjoram. Add salt to taste.

SERVES 6 · Approximately 90 to 110 calories each serving

Chocolate Fruit Fondu

½ cup chocolate bits
2 tablespoons sugar
⅓ cup evaporated milk, undiluted

⅓ cup fresh milk
½ teaspoon ground cinnamon
½ teaspoon instant coffee powder
6 pears

Place the chocolate bits, sugar, evaporated milk, fresh milk, cinnamon and instant coffee powder in a saucepan. Cook over low heat, stirring constantly, until the sauce is smooth. Pour the hot sauce into 6 tiny cups or custard cups, and place each cup on a dessert plate. Peel and core the pears, and cut each one into 8 slices. Divide the slices among the plates. Serve immediately. Each guest dips the slices of pear into the hot sauce. The hot sauce combines well with the cold fruit. Do not peel the pears too far ahead lest they start to turn brown.

SERVES 6 · Approximately 170 to 185 calories each serving

13

Asparagus Vinaigrette (hot or cold, fresh or canned, with low-calorie vinaigrette dressing)
* Viennese Chicken Livers, Onions and Apples
Low-calorie Rice
* Peppermint Pineapple
Tea or Coffee with Approved Artificial Sweetener and Skim Milk

Viennese Chicken Livers, Onions and Apples

2 large or 3 medium-size yellow onions, sliced thin
6 tablespoons butter
2 large apples, peeled, cored, and cut into 12 slices each
2 teaspoons sugar
2 pounds chicken livers
¼ cup flour
1 cup chicken stock

⅔ cup dry vermouth
Salt and pepper

Sauté the onions in 1 tablespoon of the butter, stirring very frequently, until they are tender. Remove the onions and reserve. In the same pan, sauté the apples in 1 tablespoon of the butter until almost tender. Sprinkle with the sugar and continue to cook until glazed and very tender. Remove and reserve. Dry the livers thoroughly, dust with the flour, and sauté over high heat in the remaining 4 tablespoons butter until the livers are brown. Add the stock and vermouth and cook, stirring constantly, until the sauce thickens. Replace the onions and apples in the pan and heat together. Add salt and pepper to taste. Serve immediately.

SERVES 6 · Approximately 440 to 470 calories each serving

Peppermint Pineapple

- 4 cups diced ripe pineapple
- 2 tablespoons green crème de menthe
- 2 tablespoons sugar
- 1 package (5 cents worth) green mint-flavored hard candies, crushed
- Mint leaves

Toss the pineapple with the crème de menthe and the sugar. Marinate in the refrigerator for 2 hours or more, stirring the fruit occasionally. Spoon into 6 small dessert dishes or wineglasses. Sprinkle the crushed mints on top, garnish with mint leaves, and serve immediately.

SERVES 6 · Approximately 90 to 100 calories each serving

14

Cantaloupe Rings Laced with Port
* *Spicy Shell Steaks*
French Bread (1 small slice for each person)
Watercress
* *Marinated Peaches*
*Tea or Coffee with Approved Artificial Sweetener
and Skim Milk*

Spicy Shell Steaks

- 1 tablespoon oil
- 2 tablespoons butter
- 6 boneless shell steaks, 7 ounces each, about ⅓ inch thick
- Salt and coarse black pepper
- 1 large lemon, halved
- 1 teaspoon dry mustard
- 2 tablespoons Worcestershire sauce
- 2 tablespoons minced parsley
- 2 tablespoons minced chives

Heat a large heavy skillet and put into it the oil and half of the butter. Season one side of the steaks with salt and pepper and place them, seasoned side down, in the skillet. Reduce the heat a little and sauté the steaks for 2 minutes. Turn and sauté the other side for 2 minutes longer. Remove the steaks and turn off the heat. Insert a fork in the lemon and twist it to release the juice into the skillet. Add the remaining butter, the mustard and Worcestershire sauce and blend with the lemon juice. Replace the steaks, baste with the pan juices, and heat over very high heat for just a few seconds. Transfer the meat and sauce to a serving platter or serve directly from the skillet. Sprinkle the parsley and chives over all.

SERVES 6 · Approximately 400 to 425 calories each serving

Marinated Peaches

¼ cup orange juice
2 tablespoons B & B (Benedictine and Brandy)
2 tablespoons sugar
1 teaspoon lemon juice
6 large ripe peaches

Mix the orange juice, B & B, sugar and lemon juice in a large bowl. Scald the peaches, slip off the skins, and cut the fruit into medium-thick slices. Place the peaches in the bowl and toss to coat the slices with the marinade. Cover the bowl tightly and chill for 1 hour before serving.

SERVES 6 · Approximately 120 to 135 calories each serving

15

Melon Balls in Melon (Scoop out melon balls down center of melon, invert balls in holes.)
* *Ed Giobbi's Chicken with Mussels*
Italian Bread (1 small slice for each person)
Escarole
* *Strawberries Diane*
Tea or Coffee with Approved Artificial Sweetener and Skim Milk

Ed Giobbi's Chicken with Mussels

2 tablespoons olive oil (This is less than the original quantity, but will do well.)
6 chicken quarters (all white meat, all dark meat, or some of each)
4 garlic cloves, unpeeled

SWEET DINNERS

¼ teaspoon dried orégano
¼ teaspoon dried sweet basil
½ teaspoon dried rosemary
2 cups dry white wine
1 pound fresh tomatoes, or 1-pound can Italian tomatoes, chopped into coarse pieces
1 green pepper, seeded and sliced thin
¼ cup minced Italian parsley
2 pounds mussels in shells
Salt and pepper

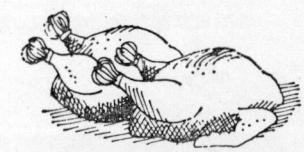

Heat the oil in a large skillet and brown chicken over high heat. Add the garlic, orégano, basil, rosemary and wine. Reduce heat to medium and cook for 5 minutes. Heat the tomatoes and pepper in a saucepan and add to the chicken with the parsley. Reduce heat to low, cover, and simmer for 30 minutes.

Scrub mussels thoroughly under cold running water and add them to the chicken. Raise heat to medium, uncover, and cook for 30 minutes longer, until chicken is tender. Remove chicken and mussels to a serving platter and keep warm. Remove and discard garlic cloves, if desired. If the sauce is too watery, reduce it over high heat. Add salt and pepper to taste. Pour over the chicken and serve immediately.

SERVES 6 · Approximately 365 to 390 calories each serving

Strawberries Diane

4 cups strawberries
2 teaspoons kirsch
1 tablespoon strawberry jam
4 eggs, separated
½ cup sugar

Hull the strawberries, wash and drain them, and allow them to dry thoroughly. About 30 minutes before serving time, mix the kirsch and the jam, spoon over the berries, and toss them gently. Divide among 6 dessert dishes. Beat the egg yolks, gradually add half of the sugar, and continue beating until the mixture is thick and light. Spoon over the berries. Beat the egg whites until foamy, gradually add the remaining sugar, and beat until very thick and shiny. Spoon over the egg-yolk mixture. Chill for 30 minutes before serving.

SERVES 6 · Approximately 165 to 180 calories each serving

16

Blender Soup Argenteuil
Cold Poached Halibut with Tiny Shrimps
Sweet Cucumber Slices (Slice cucumbers medium-thick. Dress with salt, pepper, a touch of vinegar and oil, enough sugar to make the sweetness apparent.)
Apple Soufflés à la Russe
Tea or Coffee with Approved Artificial Sweetener and Skim Milk

Blender Soup Argenteuil

- 2 pounds asparagus
- 2 large tomatoes, peeled, seeded, and chopped
- 5 cups well-seasoned chicken stock
- 1 teaspoon dried basil
- 2 tablespoons flour
- 3 tablespoons sour cream
- Salt and pepper

Break off the asparagus stalks as far down as they will snap off easily. Peel the stalks with a vegetable peeler, and cut them into 1-inch pieces. Put the asparagus, tomatoes, chicken stock and basil in a saucepan, and bring to a boil. Reduce the heat, cover the saucepan, and simmer for 20 minutes, or until the vegetables are very tender. Purée, a portion at a time, in an electric blender. A blender is necessary to achieve the velvety texture that this soup should have. Mix the flour and sour cream, add a little of the hot soup, then pour the mixture into the saucepan. Cook over medium heat, stirring constantly, until the soup thickens. Add salt and pepper to taste.

SERVES 6 · Approximately 85 to 100 calories each serving

Cold Poached Halibut with Tiny Shrimps

1 pound fish heads and bones
1 large onion, chopped
2 carrots, scraped
2 parsley sprigs
4 peppercorns
Salt
⅓ cup dry white wine
6 halibut steaks, each about 7 ounces, cut from the tail end
1 can or jar (about 2½ ounces) cooked tiny shrimps
¼ cup sour cream
¼ cup low-calorie Thousand Island dressing

Put the fish heads and bones, the onion, carrots, parsley, peppercorns, ¼ teaspoon salt, 2 cups water, and the wine in a saucepan. Bring to a boil, reduce the heat, cover, and simmer for 30 minutes. Uncover, raise the heat, and cook rapidly until reduced to two thirds. Strain into a shallow skillet just large enough to hold the fish in a single layer. Remove and reserve the carrots. Bring the stock to a boil, add the fish, and reduce the heat. Cook the fish in barely simmering liquid for approximately 8 minutes; turn carefully and simmer for 5 minutes longer, or until the fish flakes easily. Cool a little, then remove the skin and bones. Cool the fish in its stock. Drain and place on a platter or on individual plates. Slice the reserved carrots and arrange the slices alternately with the shrimps, slightly overlapping, down the center of each piece of fish. Mix the sour cream and low-calorie salad dressing and serve separately.

SERVES 6 · Approximately 275 to 295 calories each serving

Apple Soufflés à la Russe

1½ pounds apples (preferably MacIntosh)
¼ cup water
1 teaspoon vanilla extract
4 egg whites
½ cup plus 1 tablespoon sugar

Peel and core the apples and dice them. Put them in a saucepan with the water, cover, and cook over medium heat until you can mash them. (If the apples are dry, add water.) Mash them, add vanilla, and set aside. Beat the egg whites until foamy. Gradually add ½ cup sugar, beating constantly until the meringue is thick and glossy. Fold the meringue into the mashed apples, and spoon into 6 buttered individual casseroles or glass baking dishes. Sprinkle the remaining sugar on top. Bake in a preheated 375°F. oven for 15 minutes, or until the soufflés have puffed and the tops look crusty. Serve immediately.

SERVES 6 · Approximately 180 to 195 calories each serving

17

Ripe Tomato Soup
Sweetbreads Baumanière
Parsleyed Peas and Cucumbers
Strawberries in Strawberry Glaze (Purée the less desirable berries, flavor with sugar or artificial sweetener, and toss with remaining berries.)
Tea or Coffee with Approved Artificial Sweetener and Skim Milk

Ripe Tomato Soup

- 1 large onion, minced
- 1 teaspoon bacon drippings
- 1 medium-size carrot, scraped and minced
- 1 celery rib, scraped and minced
- 2 pounds very ripe tomatoes, peeled, seeded, and chopped
- 2 tablespoons flour
- 1 cup skim milk, at the boiling point
- 1 teaspoon sugar
- 1 tablespoon Maggi extract
- 1 teaspoon salt
- 2 tablespoons catsup

In a large heavy saucepan, sauté the onion in the bacon drippings for 2 minutes. Add the carrot and celery, cover, and simmer over medium heat for 15 minutes, or until the vegetables are tender but still slightly crisp. Purée the tomatoes in an electric blender or in a food mill. Sprinkle the flour over the sautéed vegetables and cook, stirring constantly, for 1 minute. Add the tomatoes and cook until thickened. Add a little of the tomato mixture to the hot milk. Gradually pour back into the tomato purée, stirring constantly over low heat until blended. Add the remaining ingredients and heat for 1 minute. Adjust seasonings.

SERVES 6 · Approximately 60 to 80 calories each serving

Sweetbreads Baumanière

- 3 to 3½ pounds untrimmed veal sweetbreads
- 1 cup minced mushrooms
- ½ tablespoon butter
- ⅓ cup heavy cream
- 2 tablespoons Madeira
- ¼ cup minced lean ham
- 1 cup fine-diced breast of chicken
- ¼ cup chopped pitted green olives

8 drops of Tabasco
Salt and pepper
1 tablespoon fine dry bread crumbs

Parboil and trim the sweetbreads (see Index, Sweetbreads Grand Hôtel de Souillac). Dice the sweetbreads. In a heavy saucepan, over high heat, sauté the mushrooms in the butter for 2 minutes, stirring constantly. Remove from the heat and stir in the cream and Madeira. Add the sweetbreads, ham, chicken and olives. Finally, add the Tabasco, and salt and pepper to taste.

Divide the mixture among 6 individual baking dishes and dust the tops with bread crumbs. Bake in a preheated 400°F. oven for 10 to 15 minutes, or until piping hot. Serve immediately.

SERVES 6 · Approximately 250 to 275 calories each serving

Parsleyed Peas and Cucumbers

2 large cucumbers, peeled, seeded, and cut into bite-size pieces
1 chicken bouillon cube, crushed
¾ cup thawed frozen peas
Salt and pepper
2 tablespoons minced parsley

Put the cucumbers and crushed chicken bouillon cube into a saucepan. Cook, covered, over low heat for about 20 minutes, or until the cucumbers are tender and translucent, stirring frequently. Add the peas and cook for 3 minutes. Uncover and cook over high heat, stirring constantly, until the peas are cooked and the pan juices almost evaporated. Add salt and pepper to taste and stir in the parsley.

SERVES 6 · Approximately 25 to 30 calories each serving

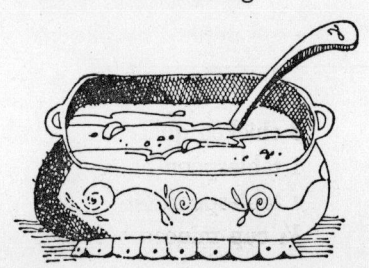

18

* Hububub (Hungarian Green-bean Soup)
* Chicken in Cider Sauce
* Lin's Water Chestnuts and Celery
*Fruits Rafraîchis (chilled fruit cup, sweetened with sugar
or light sugar syrup, flavored with kirsch)*
*Tea or Coffee with Approved Artificial Sweetener
and Skim Milk*

Hububub (Hungarian Green-bean Soup)

1 pound green beans, trimmed and cut into 1-inch pieces
1½ quarts boiling salted water
2 egg yolks, lightly beaten
3 tablespoons flour
2½ tablespoons lemon juice
⅓ cup sour cream

Cook the beans in the water until crisply tender. Drain and measure 5 cups of the liquor. Chill the beans.

In a saucepan, mix the egg yolks with the flour. Add the lemon juice and sour cream and stir until smooth. Gradually add the vegetable liquor, and simmer over medium heat, stirring constantly, until the soup thickens. Remove from the heat, cool, and chill. Adjust seasonings, add beans, and serve well chilled.

SERVES 6 · Approximately 90 to 110 calories each serving

Chicken in Cider Sauce

6 chicken quarters (from broilers)
1 tablespoon butter
1 tablespoon oil
¼ cup minced onion

½ teaspoon dried thyme
1 teaspoon salt
2 tablespoons minced parsley
1 cup apple cider
1 teaspoon flour
2 tablespoons sour cream

Brown the chicken slowly in the butter and oil in a large heavy skillet. As the pieces are browned, transfer them to a roasting pan. In the same skillet, sauté the onion for 2 minutes, stirring constantly. Add the thyme, salt, parsley and cider. Pour the mixture over the chicken. Roast, covered, in a preheated 375°F. oven for 30 to 40 minutes, or until the pieces are tender.

Transfer the chicken to a serving platter and keep warm. Mix the flour and sour cream, stir in a little of the pan juices, then return the mixture to the roasting pan. Cook over low heat, stirring constantly. Adjust seasonings. Serve the sauce separately.

SERVES 6 · Approximately 300 to 325 calories each serving

Lin's Water Chestnuts and Celery

1 celery heart
1 tablespoon vegetable oil
1 tablespoon cornstarch
1 tablespoon soy sauce
2 tablespoons thin-sliced scallions, including some of the green part
1 can (8 ounces) water chestnuts, drained and sliced thin

Trim the root end of the celery and cut off the leaves. Cut the ribs into slices 1 inch long, and cook the pieces in boiling salted water for about 10 minutes, or until just tender. Drain the celery, reserving 1½ cups of stock. Mix the oil, cornstarch, soy sauce, and a few spoonfuls of the celery stock, stirring constantly until smooth. Add the remaining stock and cook over high heat until somewhat thickened and reduced by about half. Add the drained celery, the scallions and water chestnuts. Taste, and add more salt if necessary.

SERVES 6 · Approximately 35 to 40 calories each serving

CALORIE TABLES

The amounts of the foods listed are based on the way the foods are used; for instance, milk is measured by the cup, but meat is measured by weight, or sometimes by the piece. Vegetables and fruits that are eaten whole, either raw or cooked, may be measured by the item. The measures used are the standard units: 1 cup means the standard 8-ounce measuring cup; 1 tablespoon means the standard measuring spoon which contains ½ ounce liquid. The weight of the filled cup or tablespoon will vary according to the contents, but the volume will remain the same. The calorie figures are based, in general, on information published by the United States Department of Agriculture.

DAIRY PRODUCTS

milk		
whole, fluid	1 cup	160
whole, dry	1 cup	515
skim, fluid	1 cup	90
skim, dry	1 cup	250
evaporated, unsweetened undiluted	1 cup	345
condensed, sweetened, undiluted	1 cup	980
cream		
light (coffee cream)	1 cup	505
	1 tablesp.	30
heavy (whipping cream)	1 cup	840
	1 tablesp.	55
cheese		
blue types	1 ounce	105
Cheddar types	1 ounce	105
grated	1 cup	445
cottage, creamed	1 cup	240
	1 ounce	30
uncreamed	1 cup	195
	1 ounce	25
cream	1 ounce	105
Swiss types	1 ounce	105
yoghurt	1 cup	120

MEATS*

beef		
cuts cooked with liquid	3 ounces	245

* Meat portions include both lean and fat. If all fatty portions are removed and only 3 ounces of lean meat are measured, it is possible to reduce the calories of the serving by one third to one half.

cuts cooked without liquid (roasts, etc.)		
fatter cuts	3 ounces	375
leaner cuts	3 ounces	165
cuts broiled (steaks)		
fatter cuts	3 ounces	330
leaner cuts	3 ounces	220
frankfurter, boiled	1 frank	155
hamburger, broiled		
regular	3 ounces	245
lean	3 ounces	185
heart, braised	3 ounces	160
kidney, braised	3 ounces	210
liver, fried	2 ounces	130
tongue, braised	3 ounces	210
corned beef	3 ounces	185
chipped beef	2 ounces	115
lamb		
chop, with bone, broiled, thick	1 chop	400
leg, roasted	3 ounces	235
shoulder, roasted	3 ounces	285
kidney, broiled	3 ounces	120
pork, cured		
bacon, broiled	2 slices	100
bacon, Canadian broiled	2 slices	115
ham, baked	3 ounces	320
sausage	3 ounces	405
pork, fresh		
chop, with bone	1 chop	260
cuts cooked with liquid	3 ounces	320
cuts cooked without liquid (roasts, etc.)	3 ounces	310
veal		
cutlet without bone, broiled	3 ounces	185
roast	3 ounces	230
calf's liver, fried	3 ounces	225
kidney, braised	3 ounces	140
sweetbreads, braised	3 ounces	145

POULTRY

chicken		
broiled (no skin, no bone)	3 ounces	115
breast, fried	3 ounces	155
leg, fried	2 ounces	90
canned, boneless	3 ounces	170
liver, cooked with liquid	3 ounces	140
duck, roast	3 ounces	345
goose, roast	3 ounces	380
*squab, roast	3 ounces	240
turkey, roast	1 slice	100

EGGS, shelled

raw, whole	1 egg	80
white only	1 white	15
yolk only	1 yolk	60
boiled or poached	1 egg	80
scrambled with butter	1 egg	110

FISH

bluefish, broiled	3 ounces	135
haddock, fried	3 ounces	140
mackerel, broiled	3 ounces	200
perch, breaded and fried	3 ounces	195
salmon, baked	3 ounces	120
sardines, canned in oil	3 ounces	175
shad, baked	3 ounces	170
swordfish, broiled	3 ounces	150
tuna, canned in oil	3 ounces	170

*Rock cornish game hens are similar in calorie count to squabs.

SHELLFISH

clams, raw	3 ounces	65
canned	3 ounces	45
crab meat, fresh, cooked, or canned	3 ounces	85
lobster, fresh, cooked	3 ounces	82
mussels, raw	3 ounces	80
*oysters (selects), raw	1 cup	160
canned	3 ounces	65
shrimps, raw	3 ounces	78
canned	3 ounces	100

VEGETABLES

asparagus, cooked pieces	1 cup	35
beans		
green, cooked in water	1 cup	30
lima, cooked in water	1 cup	180
dried, cooked	1 cup	260
wax, cooked in water	1 cup	30
white, dried, cooked	1 cup	310
bean sprouts, raw	1 cup	30
beets, cooked diced	1 cup	50
broccoli, cooked	1 cup	40
Brussels sprouts, cooked	1 cup	45
cabbage, raw, shredded, plain	1 cup	25
cooked	1 cup	35
carrots, raw	1 carrot	20
raw, grated	1 cup	45
cooked diced	1 cup	45
cauliflower, cooked	1 cup	25
celery, raw	1 rib	5
pieces, diced	1 cup	15
celery knob, raw	3 ounces	34
corn, cooked	1 ear	70
canned	1 cup	170
cucumber, raw	1 cucumber	30
endive, raw	10 leaves	5
kale, cooked	1 cup	30
lettuce, raw		
Boston types	1 head	30
Iceberg types	1 head	60
mushrooms fresh, raw	3 ounces	24
canned	3 ounces	15
okra, cooked	8 pods	25
onions		
raw, medium size	1 onion	40
cooked	1 cup	60
green (scallions)	6 onions	20
parsley, raw, chopped	1 tablesp.	1
peas		
fresh, cooked	1 cup	115
canned	1 cup	165
dried, cooked	1 cup	250
pepper, green, raw	1 pod	15
pimento, canned	1 pod	10
potatoes (3 per pound raw)		
baked, peeled	1 potato	90
boiled, peeled	1 potato	105
peeled, boiled	1 potato	80
French fried	10 pieces	155
mashed, with milk and butter	1 cup	155
potato chips	10 chips	115
pumpkin, canned	1 cup	75
radishes, raw	4 radishes	5

*These figures apply to Eastern oysters only. Pacific oysters have about one third more calories for the same weight or volume.

spinach, fresh, cooked	1 cup	40
squash		
*summer, cooked, diced	1 cup	30
winter, baked, mashed	1 cup	130
sweet potatoes		
baked, peeled	1 sweet	155
boiled, peeled	1 sweet	170
candied	1 sweet	295
canned	1 cup	235
tomatoes, raw	1 tomato	35
canned	1 cup	50
turnips, cooked, diced	1 cup	35

FRUITS

apples, raw	1 apple	70
applesauce, canned		
sweetened	1 cup	230
sweetened artificially	1 cup	100
apricots, raw	3 apricots	55
canned halves with syrup	1 cup	220
dried, uncooked	1 cup	390
**avocado (13 ounce)	½ avocado	160
banana, raw	1 banana	85
blackberries, raw	1 cup	85
blueberries, raw	1 cup	85
cantaloupe, raw	½ melon	60
cherries		
sweet, raw	1 cup	80
sour, canned in syrup	1 cup	230
dates, pitted	1 cup	490
figs, fresh, raw	3 figs	90
dried	1 fig	60
grapefruit, white	½ grapefr.	55
pink	½ grapefr.	60
sections	1 cup	75
canned in syrup	1 cup	175
grapes		
slip skins	1 cup	65
adhering skins	1 cup	95
oranges, fresh		
California	1 orange	60
Florida	1 orange	75
peaches, fresh		
whole	1 peach	35
slices	1 cup	65
canned halves in syrup	1 cup	200
dried, uncooked	1 cup	420
frozen	12-oz. pk.	300
pears, fresh	1 pear	100
canned halves in syrup	1 cup	195
pineapple		
raw, diced	1 cup	75
canned, crushed	1 cup	195
plums, fresh	1 plum	25
canned with syrup	1 cup	205
prunes, dried	4 prunes	70
cooked, unsweetened	1 cup	295
raspberries	1 cup	70
rhubarb, cooked, sweetened	1 cup	385
strawberries	1 cup	55
tangerines	1 tangerine	40
watermelon	1 wedge	115

NUTS, shelled

almonds	1 cup	850
Brazil nuts	1 cup	915
cashews	1 cup	760
coconut, fresh	1 cup	335
dried, shredded	1 cup	340
hazelnuts	1 cup	906
peanuts, roasted, salted	1 cup	840
chopped	1 tablesp.	55

*Zucchini is similar to summer squash.

**California varieties are more caloric.

CALORIE TABLES

peanut butter	1 tablesp.	95
pecans, halves	1 cup	740
chopped	1 tablesp.	50
walnuts		
black, chopped	1 cup	790
English, halves	1 cup	650
chopped	1 tablesp.	50

GRAINS

barley, uncooked	1 cup	710
corn grits (hominy), cooked	1 cup	120
cornmeal, whole ground	1 cup	420
corn cereals, cold	1 ounce about	100
oats, oatmeal, cooked	1 cup	130
oat cereals, cold	1 ounce	115
rice, cooked	1 cup	185
rice cereals, cold	1 cup about	100
wheat flour	1 cup	400
wheat germ	1 cup	245
wheat cereals, cold	1 oz. about	100
macaroni, cooked *al dente*	1 cup	190
noodles, with egg, cooked	1 cup	200
spaghetti, cooked	1 cup	155

BREADS

Boston brown	1 slice	100
cracked-wheat	1 slice	60
French	1-lb. loaf	1,315
Italian	1-lb. loaf	1,750
rye	1 slice	55
white, enriched	1 slice about	60
unenriched	1 slice about	60
whole-wheat	1 slice	55
bread crumbs, dry grated	1 cup	345
crackers		
graham	4 small	55
rye wafers	2	45
saltines	2	35
biscuits	1 biscuit	140
muffins	1 muffin	140
rolls, nonsweet	1 roll	115
sweet	1 roll	135
pancakes	1 pancake	60
waffles	1 waffle	210

BEVERAGES

apple juice	1 cup	120
apricot nectar	1 cup	140
coffee, plain	1 cup	2
cranberry juice cocktail	1 cup	160
grapefruit juice fresh	1 cup	95
canned, sweetened	1 cup	130
frozen concentrate, undiluted	6-ounce can	300
grape juice	1 cup	165
lemon juice	1 cup	60
	1 tablesp.	5
lime juice	1 cup	65
limeade frozen concentrate, undiluted	6-ounce can	410
orange juice fresh	1 cup	115
canned, unsweetened	1 cup	120
frozen concentrate, undiluted	6-ounce can	330
peach nectar	1 cup	120
pineapple juice, canned	1 cup	135
tangerine juice canned, unsweetened	1 cup	105
frozen concentrate, undiluted	6-ounce can	340

tea, plain   1 cup   1
tomato juice   1 cup   45

BEVERAGES ALCOHOLIC

beer   1 cup   104
*distilled spirits
  gin   1 ounce   80
  rum   1 ounce   100
  whiskey   1 ounce   100
liqueurs
  anisette   1 ounce   111
  Benedictine   1 ounce   112
  Cherry Heering   1 ounce   80
  crème de cacao   1 ounce   101
  crème de menthe   1 ounce   110
  Curaçao   1 ounce   100
  kirsch   1 ounce   83
  triple sec   1 ounce   83
**wines
still red wines   ½ cup   96
still white wines
  dry   ½ cup   90
  sweet   ½ cup   116
sparkling wines   ½ cup   116
Madeira   ½ cup   160
port   ½ cup   200
sherry   ½ cup   160
vermouth, dry   ½ cup   136
  sweet   ½ cup   180

* With distilled spirits, the higher the proof, the higher the caloric value.

** In general the higher the alcoholic content of wine, the higher the caloric value; however, sweeter wines are higher in calories than drier wines, so some sweet wines with low alcoholic content are very high in calories.

FATS AND OILS

butter 2 sticks   ½ pound   1,625
                       1 tablesp. 100
  1 standard pat   (64 per lb.) 50
margarine 2 sticks   ½ pound   1,635
                       1 tablesp. 100
  1 standard pat   (64 per lb.) 50
vegetable fat   1 cup   1,770
                       1 tablesp. 110
corn oil   1 tablesp. 125
olive oil   1 tablesp. 125
peanut oil   1 tablesp. 124

MISCELLANEOUS ITEMS

chocolate,
  unsweetened   1 ounce   145
cornstarch   1 tablesp. 30
French dressing   1 tablesp. 60
gelatin,
  unflavored   1 tablesp. 35
honey   1 tablesp. 65
mayonnaise   1 tablesp. 110
sugar, granulated   1 cup   770
                       1 tablesp. 45
sugar, brown   1 cup   820
                       1 tablesp. 50
sugar,
  confectioners'   1 cup   495
                       1 tablesp. 30
vinegar   1 tablesp. 2
yeast
  compressed,
    1 package   (⅔ ounce)   17
  active dry,
    1 package   (¼ ounce)   20

INDEX

Apple(s)
  and Banana Fluff, 172
  and Beets Smitane, 138
  Cake, Spicy, 176
  with Celery, Baked, 147
  and Chicken Livers and Onions, Viennese, 195
  Soufflés à la Russe, 202
Apricot Meringue Noodles, 152
Artichoke, cold, with low-calorie dressing, 139
Asparagus
  Blender Soup Argenteuil, 200
  Fresh, and Smoked Salmon, 66
  Ham Rolls Argenteuil, 31
  Hong Kong, 84
  Vinaigrette, 195
Aspic Dishes, *see also* Jellied Desserts
  Celery Root on a Bed of Shimmering Aspic, 33
  Chicken Livers in Aspic, 114
  Clam Coquilles, Jellied, 46
  Egg en Gelée with Vermouth, 52
  Fruit and Vegetable Mold, 61
  Horseradish Ring, Shortcut, 120
  Salmon Mold, 50
  Tomato Mold, Jellied, 38

Austrian Sauerkraut, 131

Bacon, Canadian, Endive with, 18
Bacon and Oatmeal Vegetable Soup, 45
Banana and Apple Fluff, 172
Bass with Tomatoes and Mushrooms, Baked, 128
Bean(s)
  Green-Bean Soup, Hungarian (Hububub), 205
  Green Beans and Tomatoes, 84
  Three Beans Cathay, 82
  Wax-Bean Salad, 100
Bean Sprouts, with soy sauce, 179
Beef
  Boiled, in Dill Sauce, 102
  Cantaloupe Dolma, 69
  Fillet of, Bordelaise, 95
  Orientale, 179
  Pot Roast with Sauerkraut, 192
  Pot Roast, South-of-the-Border, 153
  Shell Steaks, Spicy, 197
  Tongue in Piquant Sauce, 108
Beets and Apples Smitane, 138
Bibb Lettuce Mimosa, 188
Brains, Calves', Piquant, 184
Bratwurst Soup, 72

Breads and Toasts
  Chive Fingers, 46
  Muffin Strips, 42
  Neapolitan Toasts, 44
  Oatmeal Rounds, 165
  Sesame Slices, 133
  see also Special Treats
Broccoli Amsterdam, 89

Cabbage and Noodles, Hungarian, 150
Cabbage, Stuffed, Swedish, 137
Cake and Torte
  Apple Cake, Spicy, 176
  Hazelnut Torte, 134
  Spongecake, Chocolate, 156
  Sunshine Cake, 129
  Vanilla Butter Cake, 160
  White Chiffon Layer Cake, 126
Cantaloupe Dolma, 69
Carrie Beck's Cucumber Salad, 21
Carrots Flamande, 104
Carrots, Orange, 183
Cauliflower, Chilled, with low-calorie dip, 71
Cauliflower, Italian Style, 118
Celery
  with Apples, Baked, 147
  Celery-Stuffed, 128
  Fringed, 194
  and Mushrooms, Dutch, 155
  and Tomatoes, Farmhouse Style, 91
  and Water Chestnuts, Lin's, 206
Celery Root on a Bed of Shimmering Aspic, 33
Cheese Dishes
  Celery-Stuffed Celery, 128
  Cheese-Creamed Spinach, 173
  Cottage, Canapés on Cucumber Rounds, 103
  Cottage, Pie, Creamy, 80
  Cottage, Watermelon Molds, 65
  Liptauer Tomato, 58
  Pineapple Cheese, 185
  Polish Knedle, 166
  and Radish Open Sandwich, 50
  Sauce (Gjetost), 164
  Strawberry Blossoms, 94
Cherries, Black, and Fresh Peaches in Champagne, 89
Chicken
  Baked, Italiano, 97
  Breast of, Country Captain, 171
  Breast of, Fricassee, 81
  Broth with Pastina, 145
  in Cider Sauce, 205
  Livers in Aspic, 114
  Livers, Brochette of, 71
  Livers, Onions and Apples, Viennese, 195
  and Melon Sagaro, Summer, 188
  Most Elegant, 146
  with Mussels, Ed Giobbi's, 198
Chive Fingers, 46
Chocolate Fruit Fondu, 194
Chocolate Spongecake, 156
Clam Coquilles, Jellied, 46
Clam and Tomato Sauce with Linguine, 142
Claret Consommé, 86
Conch Chowder, Palm Beach, 49
Consommés, see Soup
Coquille of Halibut and Scallops, 64
Crab Coquilles, 20
Crabmeat, Tomato Stuffed with, 21
Cranberry Freeze, 177
Cranberry Juice with Lime, 69
Crêpes
  Apricot Meringue Noodles, 152
  Basic, 189

INDEX

Crêpes (cont'd)
  Gossamer, Filled, 189
  Manicotti Blintzes, 47
  à la Mode with Orange Sauce, 155
  Ratatouille, Sheila Stone's, 53
  Soufflés Vert Galant, 148
  Sweet, 153
Crudités, 161
Cucumber(s)
  Cream of, Creamless, 59
  and Pasta Shells, 144
  and Peas, Parsleyed, 204
  Salad, Carrie Beck's, 21
  Soup, 111
Curry Accompaniments, 182
Curry of Lamb, Delicate, 181

Dijon Mustard Sauce, 63
Dumplings (cheese), Polish Knedle, 166
Dutch Mushrooms and Celery, 155

Ed Giobbi's Chicken with Mussels, 198
Egg(s)
  and Celery Root on a Bed of Shimmering Aspic, 33
  en Gelée with Vermouth, 52
  in a Nest, 30
  Omelet, Jelly, 60
  Omelettes Soufflés with Raspberries, 98
  Poached, 29
  — with Onion Soup Oporto, 73
  — and Squash, Layered, 28
  Salad Sandwich, 41
  Scrambled, Cowboy Style, 23
  Slices with Consommé, 119
Eggplant
  Normande, 194
  Provençal, 98
  Quiche, 25
Endive with Canadian Bacon, 18

Escarole, Braised, 90
Escarole with Rye Croutons, 79

Fish, see also names of fish
  Baked, Cachalot, 99
  Cold, in Parsley Sauce, 27
  Sweet and Sour (flounder), 186
Fizzy Fruits, 193
Flounder, Fillet of Rolled, in Tomato Cups, 119
French Loaf, Glorified, 39
Frosting, White, 127
Fruit(s)
  Fizzy, 193
  Fruited Gelatin with Vanilla Cream, 74
  in Port Wine, 101
  Rafraîchis, 205
  Red, 180
  and Vegetable Mold, 61
  see also Special Treats

Geschnetzeltes, Swiss, 149
Gossamer Crêpes, Filled, 189
Grapefruit
  Broiled, 190
  and Orange Juice Frappé, 13
  Sections Marinated in Orange Juice, 18
  Shrimps in a Grapefruit Bowl, 70
Grapes, Soufflés Bacchus, Individual, 187

Halibut
  Baked, Italienne, 115
  Poached, with Tiny Shrimps, Cold, 201
  and Scallops, Coquille of, 64
Ham Rolls Argenteuil, 31
Ham, Westphalian, with Cantaloupe Balls, 93
Harmless Nibbles, 14
Hazelnut Torte, 134
Heroes, Custom-made, 36

Hors-d'Oeuvre
  Artichoke, Cold, 139
  Cauliflower, Chilled, 71
  Celery, Fringed, 194
  Celery-Stuffed Celery, 128
  Cherry and Egg Tomatoes, 186
  Cherry Tomato Hors-d'Oeuvre, 102
  Chicken Livers in Aspic, 114
  Clam Coquilles, Jellied, 46
  Cottage-Cheese Canapés on Cucumber Rounds, 103
  Crudités, 161
  Mushrooms, Crisp-Fried, 158
  Mushrooms, Stuffed, Sienna Style, 141
  Potato Miniatures, Baked, 130
Horseradish Ring, Shortcut, 120
Hungarian Cabbage and Noodles, 150
Hungarian Green-bean Soup (Hububub), 205

Italian Orange Salad, 68

Janet Rather's Zucchini Bake, 87
Jellied Desserts
  Apple and Banana Fluff, 172
  Cottage-Cheese Watermelon Molds, 65
  Fruited Gelatin with Vanilla Cream, 74
  Melon Molds with Melon Balls, 59
  Melon Ring with Strawberries, 63
  Orange Cream Sevilla, 132
  Orange-Lemon Fromage, Swedish, 92
  Orange Pineapple Ring, 178
  Pear and Strawberry Sour-Cream Ring, 107
  Pineapple Cheese, 185
  Pineapple Strawberry Mold, 116
  Spring Mold, 182

Stained Glass Window Dessert, 191
Jelly Omelet, 60

Kidneys
  Lamb, with Spiced Lamb Steaks Indienne, 112
  Veal, Chambertin, 156
  Veal, Duc d'Anjou, 190
Knedle, Polish, 166
Kohlrabi, Magyar, 109

Lamb
  Curry of, Delicate, 181
  Leg Aladdin, 133
  and Peppers en Brochette, Grilled, 117
  Steaks, Spiced, Indienne, 112
Leeks with Chopped Egg, 157
Leeks Neuchâtel, 113
Lemon Snowballs, 165
Lettuce, Some-Like-It-Hot Salad, 115
Linguine with Clam and Tomato Sauce, 142
Lin's Water Chestnuts and Celery, 206
Liptauer Tomato, 58
Liver, Chicken, see Chicken
Lobster Stew, Baked, 161
Louisiana Shrimps, 28

Magyar Kohlrabi, 109
Manicotti Blintzes, 47
Marble Chiffon, 163
Marinara Sauce, 165
Matzoth-Ball Soup, 163
Meatballs, Bite-size, 159
Meat Patties, Norwegian, in Cheese Sauce, 164
Meats, see Beef; Lamb; Veal
Melon
  Balls in Melon, 198
  Cantaloupe Dolma, 69
  and Chicken Sagaro, Summer, 188

Melon (cont'd)
  Cottage-Cheese Watermelon Molds, 65
  Molds with Melon Balls, 59
  Ring with Strawberries, 63
Meringue Desserts
  Apricot Meringue Noodles, 152
  Scandinavian Meringues, 150
  Strawberries Diane, 199
Most Elegant Chicken, 146
Mushrooms(s)
  Bisque, 183
  and Celery, Dutch, 155
  Crisp-Fried, 149
  and Smoked-Salmon Open Sandwich, 55
  Steamed, Ruth Olin's, 96
  Stuffed, Sienna Style, 141
  on Toast Continentale, 37
  and Watercress Salad, 116
Mussel(s)
  with Chicken, Ed Giobbi's, 198
  and Parsley Sauce with Green Noodles, 135
  Stew, 67
Mustard Sauce, Dijon, 63

Neapolitan Toasts, 44
Noodles and Cabbage, Hungarian, 150
Noodles, Green, with Mussels and Parsley Sauce, 135
Norwegian Meat Patties in Cheese Sauce, 164

Oatmeal
  and Bacon Vegetable Soup, 45
  Dumplings, Spinach Soup with, 41
  Rounds, 165
  Soup, Swiss, 40
Onion(s)
  and Chicken Livers and Apples, Viennese, 195
  Glazed, in Cream, 140
  Soup with Poached Egg Oporto, 73
Orange
  Carrots, 183
  Cream Sevilla, 132
  and Grapefruit Juice Frappé, 13
  Pineapple Ring, 178
  Polka Dot Soufflés in Orange Shells, 85
  Salad, Italian, 68
  Slices, Chilled, with Pistachios, 66
Oxtail Soup, 54
Oysters under a Blanket of Cress, Baked, 22

Palm Beach Conch Chowder, 49
Parsley Sauce, 94
Pasta
  Shell Soup Renata, 43
  Shells and Cucumbers, 144
  see also Linguine; Noodles
Peach(es)
  and Black Cherries, Fresh, in Champagne, 89
  Cup, 72
  Marinated, 198
Pear(s)
  Chocolate Fruit Fondu, 194
  à la Crème, 145
  and Raspberries, 136
  and Strawberry Sour-Cream Ring, 107
Peas and Cucumbers, Parsleyed, 204
Peppermint Pineapple, 196
Peppers and Lamb en Brochette, Grilled, 117
Peppers, Sweet, Ragout, 174
Pie, Cottage-Cheese, Creamy, 80
Pineapple
  Cheese, 185
  with Mint, 13
  Orange Ring, 178

Pineapple (cont'd)
  Peppermint, 196
  and Strawberries Glacé, Flaming, 174
Polish Knedle, 166
Polka Dot Soufflés in Orange Shells, 85
Port and Pepper Berries, 105
Potato(es)
  Baked, with Caviar, 51
  Miniatures, Baked, 130
  New, 137, 151; Sprinkled with Dill, 161
  Whipped, with skim milk, 153
  and Zucchini in Foil, 126
Poultry, see Chicken; Rock Cornish Game Hens; Turkey; see also Special Treats
Profiteroles, Raspberry Cream, 162

Quiche, Eggplant, 25

Radish and Cheese Open Sandwich, 50
Raspberry(ies)
  Cream Profiteroles, 162
  with Omelettes Soufflés, 98
  and Pears, 136
Ratatouille Crêpes, Sheila Stone's, 53
Rhubarb, Spring Mold, 182
Rock Cornish Game Hens
  Filled, Victorine, 131
  Foligni, 91
  Truffled, 88
Romaine Salad Parmigiana, 135
Ruth Olin's Steamed Mushrooms, 96
Salad
  Bibb Lettuce Mimosa, 188
  Cucumber, Carrie Beck's, 21
  Escarole with Rye Croutons, 79
  Green, with Gorgonzola Dressing, 97

Mushroom and Watercress, 116
Orange, Italian, 68
Romaine, Parmigiana, 135
Some-Like-It-Hot, 115
Spinach, 133
Tuna Fish Chef's, 19
Wax-Bean, 100
Salad Dressing, Creamy, 19
Salmon
  Mold, 50
  Smoked, and Fresh Asparagus, 66
  Smoked, and Mushroom Open Sandwich, 55
Salzburg Soufflés, 110
Sandwich(es)
  Cheese and Radish, Open, 50
  Egg Salad, 41
  French Loaf, Glorified, 39
  Heroes, Custom-made, 36
  Smoked-Salmon and Mushroom, Open, 55
Sauce
  Cheese (Gjetost), 164
  Dijon Mustard, 63
  Marinara, 165
  Parsley, 94
  Tomato, 48
  Vanilla Cream, 74
Sauerkraut, Austrian, 131
Sauerkraut, Pot Roast with, 192
Scallops and Halibut, Coquille of, 64
Scampi, see Shrimps
Scandinavian Meringues, 150
Sesame Slices, 133
Sheila Stone's Ratatouille Crêpes, 53
Shellfish, see names of shellfish; see also Special Treats
Shortcut Horseradish Ring, 120
Shrimps
  in a Grapefruit Bowl, 70
  Louisiana, 28
  Marinara, 165

Shrimps (cont'd)
  Scampi, Broiled, 86
  Scampi, Stuffed, with Dijon Mustard Sauce, 62
Some-Like-It-Hot Salad, 115
Soufflés, Dessert
  Apple, à la Russe, 202
  Bacchus, Individual, 187
  Crêpes Soufflés Vert Galant, 148
  Omelettes Soufflés with Raspberries, 98
  Polka Dot, in Orange Shells, 85
  Salzburg, 110
Soup
  Argenteuil, Blender, 201
  Bratwurst, 72
  Chicken Broth with Pastina, 145
  Claret Consommé, 86
  Conch Chowder, Palm Beach, 49
  Consommé with Egg Slices, 119
  Creamless Cream of Cucumber, 59
  Cucumber, 111
  Green-bean, Hungarian (Hububub), 205
  Last-of-the-Turkey, 24
  Matzoth-Ball, 163
  Mushroom Bisque, 183
  Mussel Stew, 67
  Oatmeal, Swiss, 40
  Onion, with Poached Egg Oporto, 73
  Oxtail, 54
  Pasta Shell, Renata, 43
  Spinach, with Dumplings, 41
  Tomato Bisque on the Rocks, 61
  Tomato Broth with Peas, 32
  Tomato, Ripe, 203
  Vegetable, Bacon and Oatmeal, 45
South-of-the-Border Pot Roast, 153
Special Treats, 15
Spinach
  Cheese-Creamed, 173
  Salad, 133
  Soup with Dumplings, 41
  Spring Mold, 182
Squash, *see also* Zucchini
  and Poached Egg, Layered, 28
  Two-Tone, Sauté, 79
Stained Glass Window Dessert, 191
Stew, Lobster, Baked, 161
Stew, Mussel, 67
Strawberry(ies)
  Blossoms, 94
  Diane, 199
  Melon Ring with, 63
  and Pear Sour-Cream Ring, 107
  and Pineapple Glacé, Flaming, 174
  Port and Pepper Berries, 105
  with Raspberries, 13
  Spring Mold, 182
  in Strawberry Glaze, 202
  Two-Dollar-and-Fifty-Cent, 96
Summer Chicken and Melon Sagaro, 188
Sunshine Cake, 129
Swedish Orange-Lemon Fromage, 92
Swedish Stuffed Cabbage, 137
Swedish Veal Rolls, 106
Sweet and Sour Fish, 186
Sweetbreads, *see* Veal
Swiss Geschnetzeltes, 149
Swiss Oatmeal Soup, 40

Three Beans Cathay, 82
Tomato(es)
  Beefsteak, with Basil, 149; with salt and sugar, 192
  Bisque on the Rocks, 61
  Broth with Peas, 32

Tomato(es) (cont'd)
  and Celery, Farmhouse Style, 91
  Cherry and Egg, with seasoned salt, 186
  Cherry, Hors-d'Oeuvre, 102
  Egg in a Nest, 30
  and Green Beans, 84
  -Juice Cocktail on the Rocks, 90
  Liptauer, 58
  Mold, Jellied, 38
  Ripe Tomato Soup, 203
  Sauce, 48
  Stuffed with Crabmeat, 21
Tongue in Piquant Sauce, 108
Trout Baked in Caper Sauce, 175
Tuna Fish Chef's Salad, 19
Turkey, Last-of-the-Turkey Soup, 24
Two-Dollar-and-Fifty-Cent Strawberries, 96

Vanilla Butter Cake, 160
Vanilla Cream, 74
Veal
  Braised, in Caper Sauce, 104
  Calves' Brains Piquant, 184
  Chops, Stuffed, Braised, 125
  Chop, Sweet-Stuffed, 177
  Jerez, 83
  Kidneys Chambertin, 156
  Kidneys Duc d'Anjou, 190
  in the Manner of Restaurant Lasserre, 139
  and Mushrooms Smitane, 143
Rolls, Swedish, 106
Sweetbreads Baumanière, 203
Sweetbreads Grand Hôtel de Souillac, 151
Swiss Geschnetzeltes, 149
Timbales, Parsleyed, with Parsley Sauce, 93
Vegetable(s)
  Bacon and Oatmeal Soup, 45
  Crudités, 161
  and Fruit Mold, 61
  Harmless Nibbles, 14
  Ratatouille Crêpes, Sheila Stone's, 53
Viennese Chicken Livers, Onions and Apples, 195

Water Chestnuts and Celery, Lin's, 206
Watercress and Mushrooms Salad, 116
Watermelon Cottage-Cheese Molds, 65
White Chiffon Layer Cake, 126
White Frosting, 127

Zabaglione, 113
Zucchini, *see also* Squash
  Bake, Janet Rather's, 87
  with Poppy Seeds, 107
  and Potato in Foil, 126